Minimizing Agent Turnover

"The Biggest Challenge for Customer Contact Centers"

by

Dr. Jon Anton
Purdue University
Center for Customer-Driven Quality

and

Anita Rockwell
Director of Business Intelligence
BenchmarkPortal, Inc.

The North Star

The Big Dipper

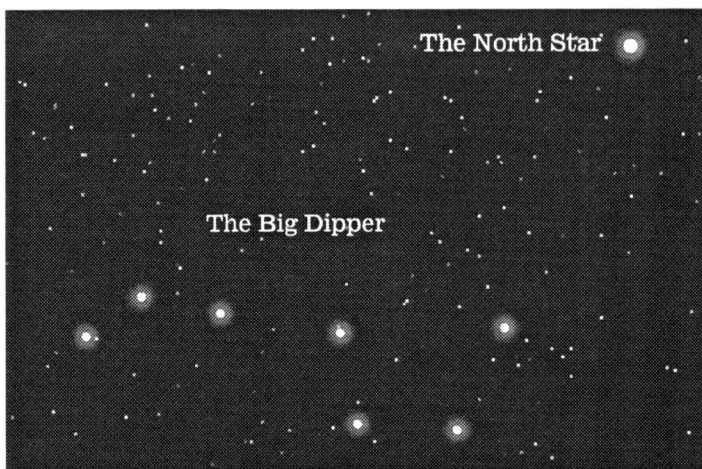

Business Navigation

Only two centuries ago, early explorers (adventurous business executives of those bygone days) were guided primarily with a compass and celestial navigation using reference points like the North Star. Today's busy executive also needs guidance systems with just-in-time business intelligence to navigate through the challenges of locating, recruiting, keeping, and growing profitable customers. The Anton Press provides this navigational system through practical, how-to-do-it books for the modern day business executive.

THE
ANTON
PRESS

2nd Edition Copyright © 2002 (16-Oct-02)

The Anton Press, Santa Maria, CA 93455
Used pursuant to license. All rights reserved

ISBN 0-9630464-2-X

Dedication

We dedicate this book to our wonderful children, and to their lifelong pursuit of knowledge and intellectual adventures.

Ben   **Casey**   **Cassidy**   **Sean**

Acknowledgements

The authors wish to express their sincere gratitude and thanks to the Simtrex Corporation for providing the research grant that made the writing of this book possible. In addition to providing a world-class suite of products for human resource development, training, and management, the executives at Simtrex have always taken a leadership role in the industry by sponsoring visionary research into the challenges and issues facing human resource managers in customer contact centers. We strongly recommend that the reader have a look at their products at: www.simtrex.com.

We especially want to thank our spouses, Suzanne and Tom, for tolerating the hours and hours we spent "burning the midnight oil" as we scoured through our research findings and transformed our ideas into words. Their strong support during the past five months kept us motivated to finish within the publisher's deadlines. In addition, we wish to thank our families for tolerating the enormous amount of personal time (nights and weekends) that our research and writing consumed in pursuing our passion to complete this book in a timely fashion. This book would not have been possible without their moral support and sacrifice.

We wish to thank Professor Richard Feinberg of Purdue University for his professional guidance and suggestions regarding our quest for answers to the many issues that impact telephone agent turnover.

We also wish to thank Mandy Schuldt, our production manager, and her team, including Debi Cloud, Susan Hampton, and Helen Ann Thomas, for their very professional work in taking our numerous drafts of the manuscript, and transforming its many words, graphs, and tables into an attractive and readable book.

Table of Contents

.

List of Figures

List of Tables

By

Craig S. Richards
CEO of Simtrex

When it comes to customer relationships, contact center agents are on the front line of business. For many companies, they are the face to the world, representing a vital touch point for customers and a critically important resource for achieving business objectives.

While few would deny that effective contact center management is one of the most important tasks for a business to get right, even fewer would argue that it's an easy objective to achieve. That's why Simtrex is proud to have sponsored Dr. Jon Anton's research into a topic that is perhaps the greatest challenge contact centers face – agent turnover.

This book represents "first-of-its-kind" research into all of the factors that contribute to agent turnover and offers practical, applicable advice for protecting the most valuable resource any contact center has, its people. Dr. Anton and his associate, Anita Rockwell, have done a marvelous job of creating a comprehensive guide to reducing agent turnover and ultimately, improving the quality of customer interactions.

As an organization dedicated to the development of top-performing contact center agents, Simtrex is delighted to be part of the visionary team that Dr. Anton leads at Purdue University's Center for Customer-Driven Quality. From his work, our industry has been rewarded with detailed best practices for effective contact center management, and this book is another example of his leadership and vision. I strongly recommend it as a "must read" for anyone charged with the task of improving customer relationships.

If you ask company executives the following questions, you will get a highly consistent set of answers:

Question	Answer
What is your greatest asset?	Our employees!
What is your primary source of competitive advantage?	Our employees!
What is the largest cost driver in your business?	Our employees!

If you ask a contact center manager the same set of questions, you will without a doubt get exactly the same answers. We went one step further and asked customer contact center managers: "What is your biggest challenge in operating your contact center?" The unanimous answer was: "Retaining great customer service agents!" In other words, these managers were saying that their biggest challenge was: "minimizing agent turnover." Ergo, the purpose of the research we conducted in writing this book was to better understand agent turnover and communicate what, realistically, you can do about it.

Most companies today have invested heavily in customer relationship management (CRM) solutions. Examples of these are: caller tracking software, sales force automation software, and customer interaction software. CRM tools have proved to be excellent for organizing and managing the data collected about a customer. However, CRM has done little to create relationships with customers.

The fact is that relationships are initiated, developed, and enhanced through a series of interactions conducted between customers (typically on the phone) and front-line telephone agents. Customers are informed about products, inquiries are answered, information exchange seals the deal, and post-sale assistance enhances the relationship. CRM is the business of front-line employees. Minimizing turnover or loss of these valuable employees is mission critical for executive management.

Agent turnover is a hot topic for several reasons:

- While turnover is a hot issue, reporting the details and root causes of turnover has been unreliable at best.

- Turnover can be very expensive. It can consume as much as 10% of your total customer contact center budget.

- Turnover causes the caller to be exposed to new-hire agents who are less knowledgeable and who don't often achieve the required caller satisfaction levels.

- New benchmark studies conducted by BenchmarkPortal and Purdue University have gone a long way to quantify the extent of the problem and its negative impact on profits.

- Now that a common language is being formed, the depth of the problem is starting to surface and is being appreciated at all levels of customer contact center management.

Figure 1 indicates that less employee turnover is considered to be the third most important issue to "fix" in order to improve call center performance. However, when you look at number one, i.e., "more productive agents," this issue is also heavily related to minimizing turnover.

Which of the following do you think would help improve your contact center?

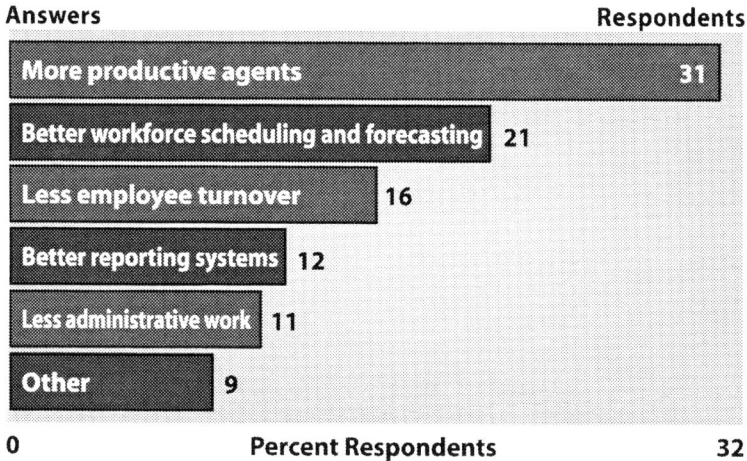

Answers   **Respondents**

Answer	Percent
More productive agents	31
Better workforce scheduling and forecasting	21
Less employee turnover	16
Better reporting systems	12
Less administrative work	11
Other	9

0   **Percent Respondents**   32

©2001 Purdue University/BenchmarkPortal, Inc.

Figure 1. This bar chart shows the answers to our question, "Which of the following do you think would help improve your contact center?" More productive agents ranks number one. Better scheduling ranks number two and less employee turnover ranks number three.

The following observations summarize the important lessons from our research into minimizing agent turnover:

- Although Human Resources represents approximately 50% to 70% of the total customer contact center budget, the hiring of new telephone agents represents, on average, 15% of the Human Resources Department budget. On the surface, turnover represents 10.5% of the total budget. For a 100-agent contact center, this figure can be as high as $300,000 per year.

- We estimate that 25% of the agents that leave your customer contact center are ineffective. The number of false starts can be reduced by more effective screening and hiring processes.

- We estimate that the remaining 75% of all turnover is the loss of effective agents, and that over 50% of this turnover can be controlled by the improvement initiatives discussed in this book.

- Telephone agent turnover must be considered in different categories, namely:
  - internal versus external
  - voluntary versus involuntary
  - functional versus dysfunctional.

- Dysfunctional turnover—the turnover of people you want to keep—results primarily from the failure of middle management to (a) provide appreciation for work done, and (b) create a supportive environment that promotes the agents feeling "in" on things.

- Since most turnover-reduction programs we studied seem to be based on raising salary and rewards, it's no surprise that these types of programs often keep the people you, in fact, want to see leave.

- There has been very limited research on turnover in general and almost no studies on causes of turnover specifically in contact centers. This book provides a multi-faceted approach to understanding turnover and its causes and provides easy-to-understand-and-apply approaches to solutions that will ultimately minimize agent turnover.

- In the contact center, agents are a vital and inextricable part of the business model success. For most companies, real profit generation is dependent on superior agent performance, which is highly impacted by agent turnover.

Background

Our approach with this book is to examine the topic of turnover from several angles. We conducted literature searches and collected what little information exists. Our goal was to clarify some aspects of turnover, such as how to define it, how to calculate it, and how to determine its cost impact to the organization. We also added some clarity to the reasons agents leave as well as to what factors cause them to stay.

The majority of our book, however, is dedicated to providing some hands-on advice on which areas within a contact center to focus on in order to have the biggest impact on retaining your talented agents. We included our best thinking and experience, as well as a composite of some of the best advice of others in the field. We like to think of this manuscript as a "how to" book for practitioners.

We also included some of the results from a survey of over 1,000 customer contact center managers. We asked them:

"What is one idea that you have implemented that actually reduced agent turnover and/or improved long-term retention?"

Figure 2 is a summary of the primary categories into which the responses to this question fell. We will explain each of these in more detail as we move through the book.

1

What is the one initiative that works best in reducing turnover?

Top Ten based on Survey	
1. Developing Retention Champions	15.5%
2. Recognition/Value/Listen	13.5%
3. Clear/Balanced Expectations/Feedback	12.2%
4. Invest in CSRs	10.3%
5. Belonging/Fun Place to Work	9.7%
6. Chance for Advancement	9.0%
7. Effective Communication	9.0%
8. Performance-based Incentives	8.4%
9. Hire Slowly/Fire Quickly	6.6%
10. Tools to Do the Job	5.8%

0   Percent of Respondents   20

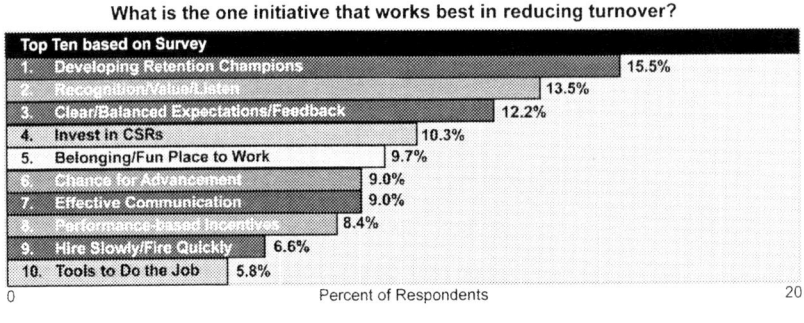

Figure 2. Initiatives that reduce turnover

We have categorized the responses by topic for easier reference and listed them later in Chapter 7. Many responses are rich with new ideas for your consideration and experimentation.

We hope you find this combination of turnover information helpful. Our greatest hope is that you will discover new insights within this book that you can apply to minimize your own turnover and thereby vastly improve your center's performance. Great agents are hard to find and even harder to keep. Yet, from all of our combined research and experience, great agents are the special ingredient that makes customer contact centers truly world-class.

Turnover Definitions

Recruiting, screening, training, and retaining good customer service representatives (CSRs) continues to be the biggest challenge facing customer contact center managers. The phenomenon of CSRs leaving their positions is commonly called "turnover," or "churn," or "attrition."

What exactly should be included in determining "turnover?" While there are different definitions for employee turnover, the basic concept is simple, namely:

"***Annual turnover*** is the total number of CSRs that leave a center in one year divided by the average number of CSRs that worked in the center during the year, typically expressed as a percentage."

Turnover includes all CSRs that leave the department for whatever reason. For example, if 33 CSRs leave a center during a twelve-month period when the average population of CSRs was 100, then there was a 33% annual turnover at that center.

Calculating Turnover

There are several ways to calculate annual turnover. In our research, we found two to be the most popular. These are described below.

Method One

$$Annual\ Turnover\ (\%) = \frac{L}{B + R - L}\ X\ 100$$

Method Two

$$Annual\ Turnover\ (\%) = \frac{L}{(E + B)/2}\ X\ 100$$

Where:
B = the number of CSRs at the beginning of the year
E = the number of CSRs at the end of the year
R = the number of new-hires during the year
L = the number of CSRs that left the center during the year.

Calculating the ROI for Turnover Improvement

At this early stage in our book, we thought it would be worthwhile to show you how to calculate, or approximate, the annual cost of whatever turnover you are currently experiencing, and the ROI for improvement initiatives. Here are the steps we suggest:

1. Determine what the costs are to recruit, test/screen, interview, and train just one new customer service representative (CSR). Using our database of thousands of customer contact centers, we have determined that the average, across industries, for bringing on a new CSR is $6,350. This cost includes all possible fees and an average applicant to hire ratio of 30 (see figure 3).

2. Determine what your true annual turnover rate is currently.

Educational Graffiti©

"People are known by the company they keep. Companies are known by the people they keep." Anonymous

Applicant-to-hire Ratio by Region

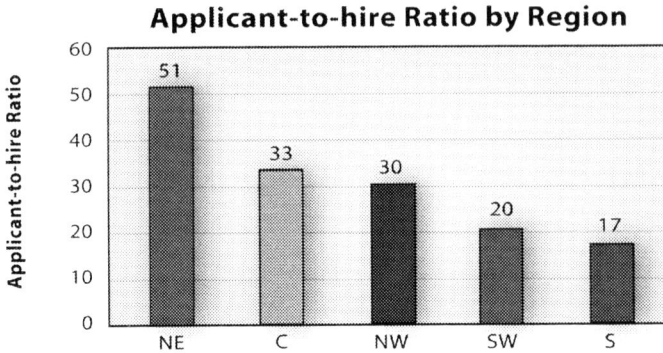

Figure 3. The above graph indicates the number of applicants that must be screened before an agent is hired. The ratio begins with the number of solicited and unsolicited resumes received, then through telephone and aptitude screening, then followed by personal interviews, resulting in an offer letter being accepted, and finally the hiring of a new agent. Obviously, from the size of the ratios, hiring is an exhaustive and expensive process.

3. The annual cost then is determined by multiplying your turnover rate by $6,350. For example, to calculate the cost of turnover for a center with 250 agents and an annual turnover rate of 20%, we multiply 250 X 20% which equals 50 new agents. The cost to recruit and training 50 new agents would be $6,350 X 50 which equals $317,500 per year.

4. If you launched an initiative to minimize CSR turnover, and this initiative cost $20,000, and let's say, it reduces annual turnover by 50%. The ROI would be calculated as follows: ((317,500 X 50%) – 20,000))/20,000 X 100 which is equal to 693%. This is obviously a very high ROI, and therefore, it should be clear that money spent on reducing turnover is well spent.

5. Let's be even more conservative. Let's say the turnover reduction initiative is only targeted to reduce annual turnover by 10%. The ROI would be calculated as follows: ((317,500 X 10%) – 20,000))/20,000 X 100 which is equal to 59%. Still not that shabby an ROI for any improvement initiative in a customer contact center.

4

Types of Turnover

Contact center turnover should be considered in several different and distinct categories, namely:

- internal turnover versus external turnover
- voluntary turnover versus involuntary turnover
- functional turnover versus dysfunctional turnover.

Internal turnover occurs when CSRs move into other positions within the company. Internal turnover can be consider either positive or negative, defined as follows:

- ◆ **Positive internal turnover** occurs within an organization when CSRs receive promotions to better-paying positions within the company. Some companies actually make an effort to routinely encourage other departments to recruit from the customer service contact center. (Let's face it, an experienced CSR makes a great employee almost anywhere in the company.) In our research, we found that the most proactive companies actually plan for a higher turnover rate within the customer contact center because of this overall corporate strategy. In these cases, the contact center needs to do "anticipatory hiring" to make sure there are enough experienced CSRs to deliver consistently high service levels.

- ◆ **Negative internal turnover** occurs when CSRs make lateral moves within the company. We found, if the internal turnover includes considerable (20% or higher) lateral movement of CSRs, it may indicate a problem. A lateral—moves means that a CSR has applied for and been hired for a position that is evaluated at the same level (pay grade) as the prior contact center position. When this happens, it generally means that the customer service pay scale has not been appropriately evaluated. For example, if a CSR seeks a position in the billing department, it may be because the new role may have less stress and offer more schedule flexibility for similar compensation.

Educational Graffiti©
"The day we screw up the people thing, this company is over." Jack Welch

External turnover occurs when CSRs leave the company entirely. There are many reasons CSRs leave organizations. External turnover can be further broken down into two categories, namely, *voluntary* and *involuntary*. We define these as follows:

♦ **External *involuntary* turnover** occurs when employees are terminated or asked to resign from the organization. Involuntary turnover is largely considered avoidable turnover, because, in most cases, it means that the wrong person was hired for the position. Later we'll discuss screening techniques that can greatly reduce the need for involuntary turnover. Our research shows that if your involuntary turnover is higher than 5%, you definitely have a "screening" problem.

♦ **External *voluntary* turnover** occurs when employees resign from their CSR position. This category has two subcategories, controllable and uncontrollable.

  • **Controllable turnover** occurs when employees resign to accept other positions or because they are not satisfied with the current employment situation. This kind of turnover can be either functional or dysfunctional described as follows:

    ○ **Dysfunctional turnover** occurs when highly valued employees voluntarily leave the contact center. Most of our turnover suggestions are targeted at this particular group. Saving these CSRs can make a big difference in the performance of your customer contact center.

    ○ **Functional turnover** occurs when marginal employees or non-producing employees decide to voluntarily leave the contact center. Great care must be taken to not make human resource changes that encourage this group to stay. When these marginal employees leave voluntarily, the company saves time and money. This type of turnover is good and should be encouraged.

- **Uncontrollable turnover** occurs when there is nothing the company could do to prevent the person from leaving. Examples of this type of turnover are: retirement, medical problems, spousal transfers, change in career goals, return to school, or leaving to care for an aging parent. From our research, this kind of turnover is reasonably constant across industries at about 1%.

In addition, we have seen that turnover varies by region of the country, as shown in figure 4.

Turnover Rate of Phone Agents by Region

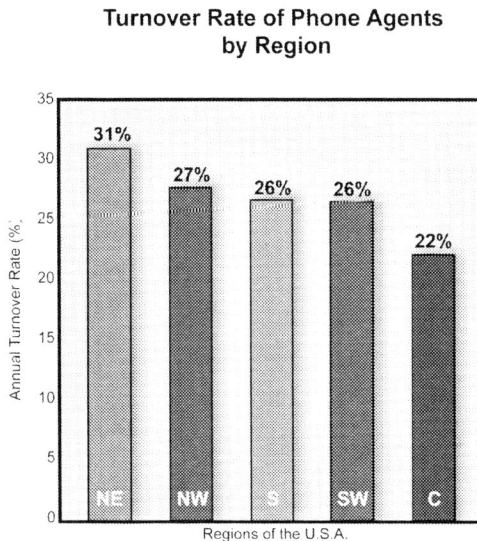

Figure 4. In this chart, we see a substantial variance in turnover by region of the U.S. with the Northeast region having the highest, and the Central region having the lowest.

Educational Graffiti©

"It's simply that the role of leadership is to serve, and the test is whether people grow. That's what underlies what we do. The reason we're in this business is to provide outstanding career opportunities. Of course, we can't do that unless we're blowing away our competitors. Do all those things, and the money just takes care of itself." Jack Lowe

"We do not produce excellence when we feel uninvolved, insignificant, and threatened." Kouzes and Posner

Employer's Level of Influence over Employee's Decisions to Stay[1]

		High	Low	
Employees Level of Control over Decisions to Leave	**High**	13% How you were treated 12% Management 8% Salary 7% Supervisor 7% Advancement opportunity 5% Workload 4% Work/life balance 4% Recognition for contributions 4% Policies and procedures 3% Career development 2% Job challenge 2% Work content 2% Working conditions 0.5% Benefits **Total: 73.5 %**	11% Retirement 2% Commuting distance 1% Start own business 0.5% Return to school **Total: 14.5 %**	
	Low		6% Illness/physical condition 6% Family circumstances **Total = 12%**	

Table 1. An example of reasons for leaving

8

Literature Search Findings on the Effects of Turnover

"Marriott reports that a 10% reduction in employee turnover has been found to correlate with a 1 to 3% decrease in lost customers and a $50 to $100 million increase in revenue."

"Sears understands the value of employee retention and satisfaction. They conducted a study and found that if employee satisfaction rose by 5%, customer satisfaction rose by 1.3%, which led to a 0.5% increase in the financial performance of the company. Given the volume of customer business now done through contact centers, that is a powerful argument for change."

"In 1999, when *Inc. Magazine* announced its annual list of the five hundred fastest growing companies in the nation, 47% of those named said that not being able to attract and keep qualified employees was their number one inhibitor to growth."

"When word gets out that an employer is committed to a working environment that honors those whom it employs, attracting and retaining high-quality performers is not an issue. When *Fortune Magazine* announces its annual list of the "100 Best Companies to Work For," organizations that make the list are bombarded with applications for employment."

The Gallup Organization recently completed some of the most extensive work on retaining talent[9], much of it contained in the book, "First, Break all the Rules." The Gallup book provides substantial back-up for the principles described in our book. It essentially quantifies the importance of the "soft side" of management as well as the critical role of the direct supervisor.

This book was the product of two mammoth research studies undertaken by the Gallup Organization over the last twenty-five years. The first study focused on employees by asking the question, "What do the most talented employees need from their workplace?"

Educational Graffiti©

"A funny thing happens when you take the time to educate your employees, pay them well, and treat them as equals. You end up with extremely motivated and enthusiastic people." Kip Tindell

"Workers always give to the organization or firm in direct proportion to what they perceive themselves receiving from it." Jack Hawley

Gallup surveyed over a million employees from a broad range of companies and asked them questions on all aspects of their working life, then dug deeper into their answers to discover the most important needs demanded by the most productive employees. The research yielded many discoveries, but the most powerful was this: "**talented employees need great managers**."

The talented employee may join a company because of its charismatic leaders, generous benefits and world-class training programs, but how long that employee stays and how productive s/he is while s/he is there is determined by her/his relationship with her/his immediate supervisor.

That discovery led to Gallup's second research study, which asked the question, "How do the world's greatest managers find, focus, and keep talented employees?"

The Gallup team conducted half hour interviews with over 80,000 managers. Some were in leadership positions. Some were mid-level managers, and some were front-line supervisors.

After running "a hundred-million questions" through their "prism," a set of twelve questions revealed consistent results in defining "what is a great place to work." These questions were as follows:

1. Do I know what is expected of me at work?

2. Do I have the materials and equipment I need to do my best every day?

3. At work, do I have the opportunity to do what I do best every day?

4. In the last seven days have I received recognition or praise for doing good work?

5. Does my supervisor or someone at work seem to care about me as a person?

6. Is there someone at work who encourages my development?

7. At work, do my opinions seem to count?

8. Does the mission/purpose of my company make me feel my job is important?

9. Are my co-workers committed to doing quality work?

10. Do I have a best friend at work?

11. In the last six months, has someone at work talked to me about my progress?

12. This last year, have I had opportunities at work to learn and grow?

The study also found the following characteristics of "bad" bosses:

1. They fail to provide feedback or ask for employee input.

2. They take credit for employees' work.

3. They renege on a promised salary, bonus or benefit.

4. They push employees while slacking off themselves.

5. They micromanage and are too controlling.

6. They insist employees routinely come in early and/or work late.

7. They turn down ideas without listening or considering them.

Purdue University Findings

Our own research underscores the importance of minimizing turnover. In figure 5, we plotted the results of a question asked of approximately 1,000 contact center professionals:

"What issues in your call center would you like to resolve now?" The aggregate answers show that turnover is high on their list.

Educational Graffiti©

"There are two kinds of organizations: those where people count and those where people don't count." Bill Guillory

11

Issues to Resolve

Reason

Be able to handle calls more efficiently	36.2%
Reduce turnover of my agents	26.3%
Reduce costs	19.4%
Find more qualified agents quickly	18.1%

0   5   10   15   20   25   30   35   40

Percent of Responses

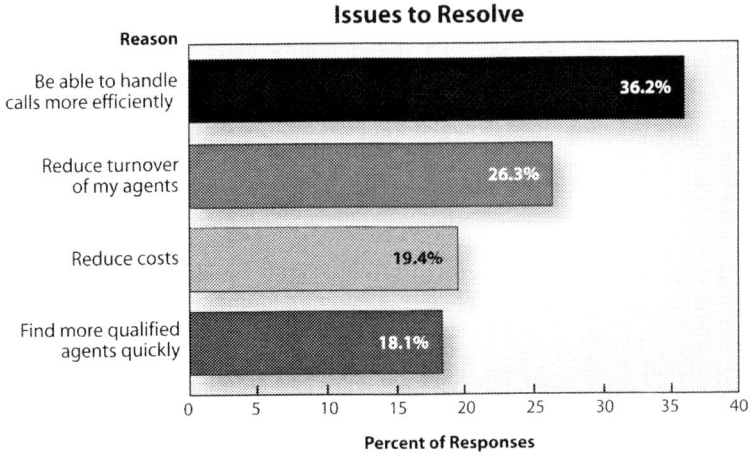

Figure 5. This bar chart shows the answers to our question, "What issues in your call center would you like to resolve now?" Being able to handle calls more efficiently is by far the most important issue with agent turnover being a close second.

Literature Search Findings on the Reasons for Turnover

In a report by the Society of Human Resource Management (SHRM), in exit interviews, they found that the top reason cited for leaving was "opportunity for advancement."[31]

The researchers mailed a survey to people who had left the company four to six months earlier. This is what they reported:

1. They didn't think the company valued their work.

2. They received too little training.

3. They were offered another job with more money.

4. They were offered another job with more responsibility.

5. They had an unfavorable relationship with their supervisor.

6. They wanted a situation that provided more growth.

7. They received little recognition for their work.

From employees still in their positions, here are the issues they were least satisfied with:

1. feeling recognized for their work
2. having a thorough orientation to the company
3. being informed of goals and performance
4. feeling fairly compensated.

In addition, the researchers also surveyed customer service representatives (CSRs) and found that the following factors were the most valued aspects of their jobs:

1. adequate compensation
2. working with people I respect
3. opportunities to learn
4. having my opinion count
5. providing service to others
6. enjoying the work I do.

Literature Search Findings on Employee Commitment

A new, nationwide survey on the attitudes of more than 7,500 workers finds that only about half of the workers polled say they are committed to their employers. Another 16% percent say they are not. The remaining 29% was neutral.[33]

In another study we found seven key factors that drive employee commitment:[27]

1. trust in leadership
2. chance to use their skills on the job
3. job security
4. competitive package
5. quality of company's products/services
6. absence of work-related stress
7. honesty and integrity of company's business conduct.

Educational Graffiti©
"Retention boils down to basic best practices. A company that engages its people at all levels and in all ways is a company that keeps them." Barbara Ettorre

Another group of researchers focused on retention. Here are the twelve most common reasons that they found as to why employees stay with a company, listed in the order of frequency:[20]

1. career growth, learning and development
2. exciting work and challenge
3. providing meaningful work that makes a difference and a contribution
4. great people to work with
5. being part of a team
6. good boss
7. recognition for job well done
8. fun on the job
9. having some level of work autonomy and a sense of control over my work
10. flexibility (for example, in work hours and/or dress code)
11. fair pay benefits
12. inspiring leadership.

The study also found that early signs of turnover risk included:

1. lack of eye contact (sign of guilt)
2. overdressing for work (interview-ready)
3. mysterious phone contacts
4. failure to attend meetings (disconnecting)
5. poor attendance (loss of commitment)
6. clean desk (change in behavior)
7. losing interest in work.

Again, our own research corroborates some of the literature suggestions about turnover. In figure 6, we plotted the demographic factors driving agent turnover. This research was conducted by "overlaying" our database of over 5,000 contact centers and all of their key performance metrics, with a demographic database owned by C.B. Richard Ellis, a large real estate company that specializes in contact center site location and call center facilities.

Demographic Factors Driving Agent Turnover

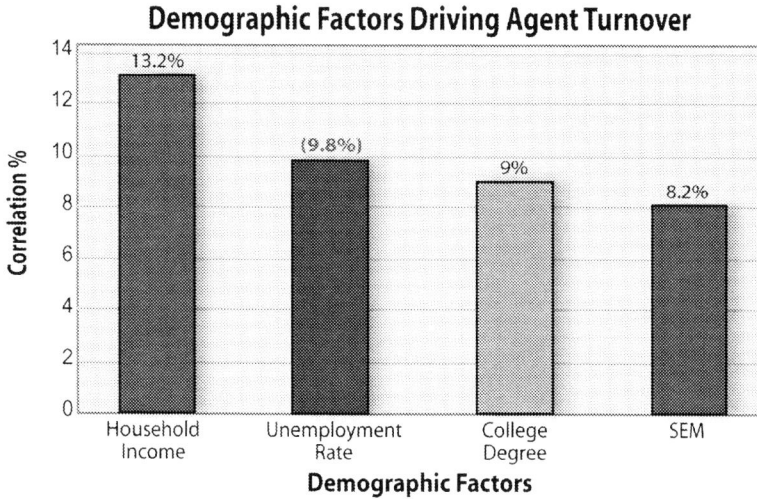

Figure 6. The above graph shows the demographic factors that have the largest statistical impact on turnover. SEM is the demographic factor that indicates the overall quality of life in a region.

Literature Search on Turnover Risk Assessment

Another study found that managers should know the answers to the following questions in order to assess the risk of turnover:[1]

1. Do you know why this person works for your company and not somewhere else?

2. Have you talked with this employee about several different career options, and does the employee perceive movement in that direction?

3. Do you know this person's number one career concern, and are you working together to address it?

4. Do you know how valuable this person's skills are in the competitive market?

5. Do you remain vigilant for any sign of fatigue or overwork, and do you take prompt supportive action to correct it?

Educational Graffiti©

"When you hire people who are smarter than you are, you prove you are smarter than they are." Anonymous

15

6. Do you have an open, trusting, respectful relationship with this person?

7. Does this employee know that he or she is fairly compensated for his or her contributions?

8. Do you know the employee's long-term goals, and are you actively supporting them?

9. Does this person's work environment meet her/his personal and professional needs?

10. Has this person's mood, physical health, and overall disposition been stable in the last six months?

11. Does this employee fit into the corporate culture?

12. Is this person's expertise critical to the organization?

13. Does this person have enthusiasm and passion for the work s/he is doing?

14. Does this employee seem satisfied with her/his work situation?

15. Does this employee know you will actively promote her/his development via training and learning opportunities?

Purdue University Findings

Once more we will refer to our own research. In tables 2 and 3 that follow, it's very interesting to see how turnover varies not only by industry segment, but also by contact center function.

Call Center Performance Metrics by Industry Segment					
Industry Segments	Once and Done (no call backs)	ATT (minutes)	ACWT (minutes)	ABN (percentage)	Annual Turnover (percentage)
Consumer Products	84.0%	3.6	2.7	7.1%	22.6%
Utilities (Electric/Gas/Water)	83.8%	4.6	2.0	5.8%	16.6%
Financial Services (Banks/Brokerages)	82.2%	2.8	2.5	5.0%	23.9%
Insurance (Life/Health/Disability)	82.2%	6.3	4.5	4.0%	29.0%
Health Insurance (HMO)	81.0%	3.1	3.2	7.4%	13.8%
Catalog	78.5%	5.4	2.1	5.0%	18.3%
Credit Card	73.0%	2.4	1.2	4.2%	46.9%
Government (Federal/State)	72.0%	5.4	1.5	8.2%	16.7%
Computers (Hardware/Software)	70.1%	9.0	10.6	5.6%	17.5%

"Once and Done" - percentage of inbound calls that were completed to the caller's satisfaction on the first call without being transferred and/or without a call back.
"ATT" - average talk time in minutes.
"ACWT" - average after-call work time in minutes.

"ABN" - percentage of inbound calls that abandon (hang up before reaching a live agent).
"Annual Turnover" - percentage of full-time agents who leave a call center in a year compared to the average total agents employed at the call center during the same year.

Table 2. Turnover varies considerably by industry with credit card centers having the largest and health management organizations the smallest.

Performance of Inbound Call Center by Function					
Call Center Functions	Talk Time (minutes)	After-Call Work Time (minutes)	First-Call Resolution (percentage)	Abandon Rate (percentage)	Agent's Turnover (percentage)
Service Dispatching	3.5	4.3	82.0%	6.3%	16.3%
Consumer Affairs	3.7	1.8	57.9%	4.4%	9.1%
Public Relations	4.0	0.0	45.0%	2.0%	4.0%
Reservations	4.3	1.7	51.9%	6.1%	43.3%
Order Taking/Tracking	4.8	3.6	76.6%	4.7%	18.4%
Inside Sales	8.1	15.5	47.4%	4.6%	13.8%
Customer Service	8.7	6.0	23.1%	4.8%	23.2%
Technical Support	8.7	9.5	65.4%	7.0%	21.0%
Pre-Sales Questions	10.3	3.9	70.1%	4.0%	19.4%
Internal Help Desk	13.4	10.0	60.5%	6.1%	16.8%
Call Routing	13.7	2.3	43.2%	4.8%	18.2%
Complaint Resolution	23.1	4.2	50.3%	3.9%	12.7%

Table 3. Turnover varies considerably by the type of calls being handled with reservations having the largest and public relations the smallest.

Educational Graffiti©

"More specifically, what people want most from their supervisors is the same thing that kids want most from their parents. They want someone who sets clear and consistent expectations, cares for them, values their unique qualities, and encourages and supports their growth and development." Gallup Poll, 1999

Introduction

What is unique about turnover in a customer contact center? While turnover is a concern in any industry, some special factors that concern contact centers are not applicable to other work environments.

If you have ever worked in a contact center, you will understand that a contact center is like a "company within a company." A contact center is fundamentally different than the core business it supports. An entirely different skill set is required to consistently deliver superior service.

Effectively managing a contact center is both an art and a science. The "science" aspect of contact center management is connected to the robust technology combined with the seemingly unlimited key performance indicators (KPIs) (also called performance metrics). There are measurements for almost everything -- from call blockage rates for incoming calls to CSR occupancy, to the percentage of the time a CSR is idle. You name it, and it is probably measured in a contact center.

The "art" of contact center management is the larger and more critical aspect and is based on the fact that the success of a contact center is almost entirely dependent on the people within it. Since between 50% and 70% of the costs of operating a contact center are tied to the personnel component, the ability of the manager to excel at all the people-related aspects can make or break the center's success (see figure 7).

Cost Allocations of Ongoing Annual Costs (in percent)

Category	Percent
Salary, benefits	57.29%
Telecommunications phone charges	9.28%
Computer hardware	5.08%
Recruiting screening, training	4.62%
Real estate (floor space)	4.37%
Telecommunications equipment	4.12%
Computer Software	3.58%
Outsourced calls	1.89%
Other	9.77%

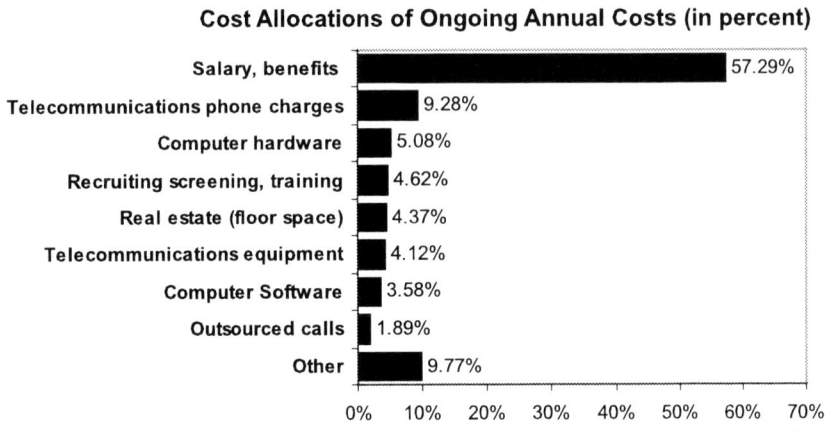

Figure 7. Contact center cost breakdown

Here are some unique factors we found that are critical for contact center management:

1. Contact centers require intense emotional capacity.

    Working in any form of customer service is a challenge and even more so in telephonic customer service. As highlighted below, a CSR's position is emotionally draining.

    > Some jobs are tough because of the physical labor involved. Customer service is heavy duty work because of the psychological energy it consumes.
    >
    > In customer service, you're working with moods, tempers, expectations and misunderstandings. You're dealing with personalities...human beings. You have to cope with their headaches, hormones and personal hang-ups. It can be a brutal job.[20]

2. Contact centers are tightly managed.

    CSRs are measured from the moment they arrive at their desks until the moment they "sign off the phones." All of their work time, such as average talk time, after call work time and idle time is measured, processed, reported on and monitored. There are time-related expectations and goals set to almost all CSR actions.

3. Contact centers are staffed primarily by women.

    In order to achieve an optimum level of employee satisfaction when working with a primarily female employee base, there are unique factors to consider. Many of these factors deal with balancing work and life. Even today, women are more likely to be responsible for coordinating childcare and managing the home. The ability to balance the job and the home can be a major factor in job satisfaction and retention.

4. Contact centers attract a mix of employee ages and types.

    To effectively manage a contact center, managers need to understand how to customize the motivational method for each agent, based on individual personality and preferences. Contact center managers also need to understand the unique differences in value sets and belief systems for several generations. The manager needs to understand group dynamics to create a cohesive team of very different individuals who may range in age from 20 to 65. Considering the wide range of interests and value sets, this is not an easy task.

5. Contact centers offer virtually no privacy.

    Contact centers typically house a large number of CSRs in a relatively small space. Almost any action or comment made by a CSR can be observed. Many contact centers have low walls surrounding the individual cubicles. Often these low walls are to enhance communication between CSRs, but they also minimize privacy and personal space. Many contact centers do not provide CSRs with personal phone lines (there may be a public pay phone in the lobby, often with a waiting line).

Educational Graffiti©

"The single most important variable in employee productivity and loyalty turns out to be not pay or perks or benefits or workplace environment. Rather, it's the quality of the relationship between employees and their direct supervisors." Anonymous

All of the previous issues have some bearing on the extent of CSR turnover. Our own research on the reasons stated by CSRs in exit interviews is shown in figure 8. It is clear that whatever "stress" is, it's the overwhelming reason for quitting as stated by exiting CSRs. The challenge for contact center managers is to focus on all those issues that create real or perceived stress for CSRs.

Reasons for Agent Turnover

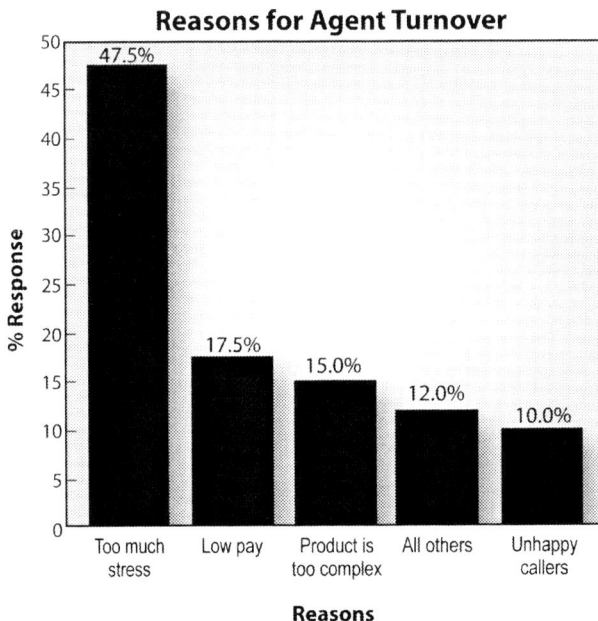

Figure 8. This chart shows the reasons for leaving as stated by telephone agents during exit interviews. It is interesting to see how much the "stress" factor impacts turnover.

Turn Managers into Retention Champions

Of all the changes a company can make to minimize turnover, turning managers into retention champions is the one to focus on for the greatest impact and longest lasting results. This is also the foundation on which our other solutions are dependent.

CSRs will not actively look for reasons to leave a contact center where the manager:

- treats them fairly
- looks out for their best interests
- advocates issues that are important to them
- operates with integrity
- tries to be flexible in finding solutions to unique situations.

We have found that once managers understand how pivotal their role is in the retention of talent, they will begin to change their focus and become a part of the solution, as opposed to often being a big part of the problem.

Retention Champions:

1. *Select them carefully*. Make sure you have the right people in these roles. Many managers may be better suited to be project managers rather than people developers.

2. *Educate them*. Share some of the overwhelming evidence that helps them appreciate the level of influence they personally have in their role as first-line leadership.

3. *Train them*. Most new managers will not know how to effectively manage in their new role. Just as they are expected to develop and commit themselves to the success of their team members, so should their direct leaders be committed to developing them as managers.

4. *Monitor them*. Develop systems to ensure that each "retention champion" is able to behave in ways that are consistent with an effective leader. For example, conducting a team survey on leadership effectiveness every quarter. Make sure the right questions are asked.

5. *Reward them*. Closely connect incentive pay or bonus dollars to their quantifiable success. Retention, or its inverse turnover, is easily quantified. Set goals for the manager and make sure they are met or exceeded.

Educational Graffiti©

"We have a belief that our guests will only receive the kind of treatment we want them to if the cast members receive that same kind of treatment from their managers." Walt Disney World Handbook

Initially, consider a scale of incentives that rewards not only exceptional retention rates, but also awards progress from the prior period.

6. *Measure and recognize them*. We have all heard, "What gets measured gets done; what gets recognized gets done even better."

7. *Be a Retention Champion to them*. Apply the same principles outlined above to them as you are their direct leader.

> **Tying manager incentive and/or bonus dollars to retention rate is critical to success.**

Once the right "people-developers" are trained and in place, watch for these behaviors as they transform into "Retention Champions":

- Selection and Hiring Process. Observe if they are more selective about who joins their team, knowing that hiring slowly (carefully) increases the odds of a successful, long-term employee.

- Orientation. Observe them making sure employees really understand how the company operates and how their role within it makes a significant contribution.

- Training and Transition. Observe them making sure the new employees receive enough training to feel competent in their role, and see if they provide a more nurturing environment until the new-hire is confident on their own.

- Expectations and Feedback. See if time is spent making sure that expectations are clear, fair and balanced and that each team member understands how each metric is measured and communicated. Observe if they consistently deliver on commitments made to each employee.

- Create a Caring Environment. See if time and energy are being spent creating "a great place for great people to work." Are they creating team spirit and a sense of belonging to increase commitment levels?

- Respect Each Individual. Observe if they are more focused on effective listening. Also, are they seeking input and acting on suggestions from the team?

- Being a Champion to the Team. Are they advocating for ways to make things better for their team? Do they recognize that taking care of employees results directly in employees taking care of the customers?

- Developing People. Are they always looking for ways to enrich and grow each member of the team? Are they dedicated to helping each person on the team move forward on their personal goals? In some cases, they may even help them determine what their goals are.

- Customized Appreciation/Recognition. Are they spending more time understanding specifically what's important to each member of their team? The manager should work to provide individual recognition that is meaningful rather than apply the same approach to the entire team. Do they freely "praise/promote" each team member?

- Communication. Observe how they focus on both formal and informal communication methods. Formally, do they make sure each employee is aware of on-going changes as they occur via the fastest and most effective methods, i.e., e-mail, voicemail and the like?

- Care of Individuals. Are they more nurturing and personally committed? Watch if they act in the best interests of individuals on their team as people first, employees second. Do they include things like trying to accommodate flexible scheduling options and being interested in what's important to each member of the team? Do they cultivate a strong level of trust with their CSR team members?

- Tools and Obstacles. Observe if they are committed to making sure that each employee has all the tools needed to be successful in the performance. Are they vigilant about removing obstacles that hinder the employee's ability to deliver results?

25

Guiding Principles for Retention Champions

We found three guiding principles that will help create the foundation for managers to become effective retention champions. They are: (a) servant leadership principles, (b) Stephen Covey's principle-centered leadership, and (c) situational leadership. We will explain them in this order in the following paragraphs.

Servant Leadership is based on a "people-first" philosophy by Robert Greenleaf.[18] The ten principles are as follows:

1. Listening
Leaders have traditionally been valued for their communication and decision-making skills. Although these are also important to the servant-leader, they need to be reinforced by a deep commitment to listening intently to others. He or she seeks to listen receptively to what is being said. Listening also encompasses getting in touch with one's own inner voice and seeking to understand what one's body, spirit and mind are communicating. Listening, coupled with regular periods of reflection are essential to the growth of the servant-leader.

2. Empathy
The servant-leader strives to understand and empathize with others. People need to be accepted and recognized for their special and unique spirits. One assumes and recognizes others for their special and unique spirits. One assumes the good intentions of co-workers and does not reject them as people, even when one is forced to accept their behavior or performance. The most successful servant-leaders are those who have become skilled, empathetic listeners.

3. Healing
One of the great strengths of servant-leadership is the potential for healing one's self and one's relationship to others. Many people have broken spirits and have suffered from a variety of emotional hurts. Although this is a part of being human, servant-leaders recognize that they have an opportunity to "help make whole" those with whom they come in contact.

4. Awareness

General awareness and especially self-awareness, strengthens the servant-leader. Making a commitment to foster awareness can be scary-you never know what you may discover.

5. Persuasion

Another characteristic of servant-leaders is a reliance on persuasion, rather than on one's positional authority, in making decisions within an organization. Rather than coerce compliance, the servant-leader seeks to convince others. This particular element offers one of the clearest distinctions between the traditional authoritarian model and that of servant-leadership. The servant-leader is effective at building consensus within groups.

6. Conceptualization

Servant-leaders seek to nurture their abilities to "dream great dreams." The ability to look at a problem (or an organization) from a conceptualizing perspective means that one must think beyond day-to-day realities. For many managers, this is a characteristic that requires discipline and practice. The traditional manager is consumed by the need to drive short-term operational goals. The manager who wishes to also be a servant-leader must stretch her/his thinking to encompass broader-based conceptual thinking.

7. Foresight

Closely related to conceptualization, foresight is the ability to anticipate the likely outcome of a situation that is hard to define, but easy to identify. One knows it when one sees it. Foresight is a characteristic that enables the servant-leader to understand the lessons from the past, the realities of the present and the likely consequence of a decision for the future. It is also deeply rooted within the intuitive mind. There hasn't been a great deal written on foresight. It remains a largely unexplored area in leadership studies, but one most deserving of careful attention.

Educational Graffiti©

"There are no tricks to becoming a good place to work, just a top-to-bottom, rock-ribbed belief that everybody in the company counts the same." Jack Lowe

8. Stewardship

Peter Block (author of *Stewardship and The Empowered Manager*)[6] defines stewardship as "holding something in trust for another." Servant-leadership, like stewardship, assumes first and foremost a commitment to serving the needs of others. It also emphasizes the use of openness and persuasion, rather than control.

9. Commitment to the Growth of People

Servant-leaders believe that people have an intrinsic value beyond their tangible contributions as workers. As such, the servant-leader is deeply committed to the growth of each and every individual within his or her institution. The servant-leader recognizes the tremendous responsibility to do everything within her/his power to nurture the personal, professional and spiritual growth of employees. In practice, this can include (but is not limited to) concrete actions such as:

- making funds available for personal and professional development
- taking a personal interest in ideas and suggestions from everyone
- encouraging worker involvement in decision-making; and
- actively assisting laid-off workers to find employment.

10. Building Community

The servant-leader senses that much has been lost in recent human history as a result of the shift from local communities to large institutions as the primary shaper of human lives. This awareness causes the servant-leader to seek to identify some means for building community among those who work within a given institution.

Stephen Covey's Principle Centered Leadership concepts are based on his book, *The Seven Habits for Highly Successful People*.[10] While all his principles help develop managers, the best retention philosophy and the one concept that makes an immediate difference is the concept of an "emotional bank account."

Covey created the concept of emotional bank accounts. An emotional bank account is a metaphor that describes the amount of trust that's been built up in a relationship; it's the feeling of safeness you have with another human being. In any relationship, trust gets built or eroded over time. Like a financial bank account, we can accumulate reserves. Trust is the cornerstone of any relationship; it builds commitment.

How are deposits made? Deposits are made:

- by being consistent in character
- by always keeping your commitments
- by telling the truth
- by looking out for another's best interest
- by giving sincere appreciation and compliments, and
- by showing genuine interest in another through active listening.

How are withdrawals made?

- by breaking promises
- by being critical
- by doing anything intentionally hurtful.

An emotional bank account can become overdrawn and the trust level deteriorates.

Emotional Bank Account
Questions that Evaluate Effectiveness

Dr. Covey highlights nine questions:
1. Willingly assists and serves people
2. Acknowledges and apologizes for mistakes
3. Is honest in interactions with people
4. Does not backbite or gossip
5. Keeps promises and honors commitments
6. Shows courtesy and respect for people
7. Does not show favoritism toward certain people
8. Helps create a positive and optimistic work environment
9. Leads by examples (i.e., "walks the talk").

Educational Graffiti©

"The greatest sources of satisfaction in the workplace are internal and emotional."
Anonymous

Emotional Bank Account Deposits

Dr. Covey highlights six major deposits:

1. Understanding the individual
2. Attending to little things
3. Keeping commitments
4. Clarifying expectations
5. Showing personal integrity
6. Apologizing sincerely when you make a mistake.

Situational Leadership is a leadership model for developing people over time so that they can reach their highest level of performance or career goal. Kenneth Blanchard developed the original model.[5] We've adapted it slightly to meet our minimizing turnover objectives, and we have used more layman's terms in our explanation.

The model is based on a recognition that while everyone is confident and competent at many things, when we attempt a new skill and/or activity, we are back to the bottom on confidence and competence because there is no prior knowledge and/or experience.

The situational leader adapts her/his style to the appropriate level based on where each individual is within the learning curve. S/he also promotes a more open atmosphere of not expecting anyone, even leadership to get things right the first time. It's "okay" to fail.

We'll use Blanchard's golf analogy to illustrate.

The approach uses four levels:

The first level is _Directive_: When someone has little or no experience and therefore has no confidence or competence with the new skill.

Golfer: The first time someone takes a lesson, the golf pro is very directive in the approach. The pro tells the student exactly how to stand, where to place his/her feet, exactly how to tee up the ball, and so on.

The next level is <u>Coaching</u>: When someone begins to understand the basic concepts of the new skill. This level helps "mold" the person to use the new skills.

Golfer: After the student has mastered the basics, the pro starts to coach on some of the next level abilities. The pro may focus on putting or chipping skills. Again, as they go through this level, the student is gaining more and more confidence as s/he gains more competence.

The third level is <u>Supporting</u>: This level is confidence building and fine tuning.

Golfer: The student is now capable of handling the majority of the aspects of the golf game. At this level, the pro will reinforce all the aspects that the student is doing correctly as well as provide pointers to correct (or fine tune) the student's game. They may discuss how to correct a hook shot or when to shift weight for certain strokes. The confidence and competence level are at a high and sustainable level.

The final level is <u>Delegation</u>: This level describes the point when the "student" or person developing a new skill is capable of using the skill on their own. They are considered to now be fully competent with the new skill.

Understanding and using this approach contributes to a culture that is supportive and in which it is safe to make mistakes. It's important to make sure everyone on the team understands the concepts so that the team can all speak the same "language."

Effective leaders do the following naturally:

- They always try to make others feel important.
- They articulate and promote a consistent vision.
- They always follow the golden rule.
- They are quick to admit mistakes.
- They do not criticize others in public.
- They stay close to where the action.

Educational Graffiti©

"If you really want people to respond to your leadership, you have to have a personal relationship with them. They need to know you're dependable and that you'll be there if they have a problem. That's personal power to me." Noreen Haffner

A Case Study on Retention

A case study in mentoring relationships.

American Express Co., the financial services behemoth headquartered in New York, plans to double its team of advisers and analysts to 20,000 over the next eight years. To accommodate that kind of growth in the face of a labor shortage, the company, known for promoting from within, is teaching its managers how to establish mentoring relationships with skilled employees. The objective is to identify rising stars, nurture their talent, and reassure them of their value before they go looking for that security elsewhere. Managers are held accountable; retention rates are considered in their performance reviews.

Verbatim comments from in-service practitioners in the Purdue Study:

"We got a new manager who listened, supported us, asked us what we thought, and asked good questions."

"The key is understanding that the biggest key to keeping good people is providing them one-on-one interaction with their boss. We use the phrase, "It's the boss, stupid!" time and again to make sure our team leaders know that people won't stay because of center level incentives if they hate their boss. People might seek out a job because of pay, benefits, etc., but if their boss makes them miserable every day, they won't stick around."

"Remembering that while we may have hired employees, that we got people instead…Meaning: Don't forget the human element."

"It's not all about pay - it's about creating an environment where the employee feels valued and part of a community."

Literature Search Findings on Managers as Retention Champions

According to research by Kepner-Tregoe, a consulting firm in Princeton, NJ, 75% of workers find leadership uninspiring, and two-thirds say management does little or nothing to address turnover.[24]

Based on 20 years of research and 60,000 exit interviews, the Saratoga Institute reports that 80% of turnover is related to unsatisfactory relationships with the boss.[32]

Literature Search Findings on Best Practices in Telephone Service

Successful organizations treat front-line workers with dignity and respect, and involve them in planning all aspects of contact center operations, especially those that impact customer service and front-line worker effectiveness. Management concern for front-line worker morale and well-being is illustrated by positive actions, such as by offering fitness centers, and child day-care centers, as well as by making personal development and stress reduction programs available to all CSRs. These are typically provided on-site, along with high-quality dining facilities that are used by everyone, from the top management to new trainees that are just beginning their customer service profession. There are no executive dining rooms at world-class operations![14]

Purdue University Findings

From our own research, we can see that retention champions have several ways of focusing on the issue. In figure 9, contact managers indicate that of the top four challenges facing them in 2001, three are CSR related, namely, (a) improving the quality of service, (b) increasing CSR productivity, and (c) reducing CSR turnover. On closer inspection, it's our opinion that the first two can be drastically improved by simply reducing CSR turnover.

Educational Graffiti©

"What if I train them and they leave? What if you don't and they stay?" Anonymous

"To get the right answer, it helps to ask the right question." Anonymous

What are the biggest challenges facing your contact center in 2001?

Answers   **Respondents**

- Improving quality of service — 23%
- Increasing agent productivity — 21%
- Integrating technologies/systems — 18%
- Reducing staff turnover — 11%
- Integrating new channels — 10%
- Reducing costs — 10%
- Other — 7%

0   **Percent Respondents**   25

©2001 Purdue University/BenchmarkPortal, Inc.

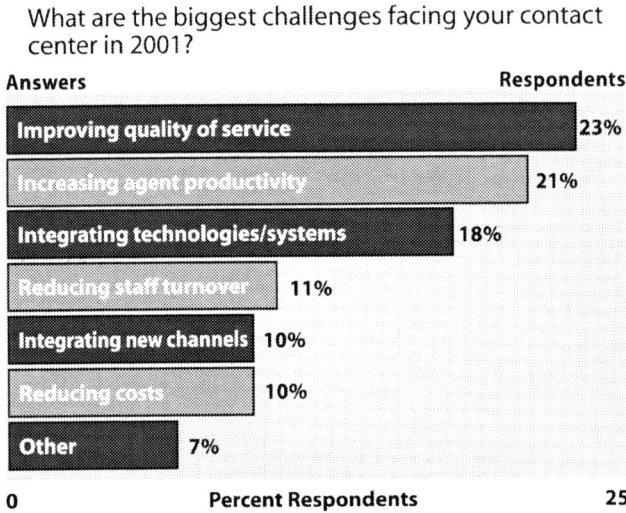

Figure 9. This bar chart shows the answers to our question, "What are the biggest challenges facing your contact center in 2001?" Reducing turnover ranks number four after such other important issues as improving quality and increasing productivity.

In conclusion, we have one more relevant piece of research. In this case, we surveyed a statistical sample of CSRs with the question, "As a telephone agent, what elements of your job are most important to you?" In figure 10 below it is clear that 92% of the respondents indicated that having "good relations with my boss" is a very important element of job satisfaction.

As a telephone agent, what elements of your job are important to you?

Answers	Percent Selected
Good relations with my boss	92%
Ongoing training	86%
Competitive compensation	75%
Advancement fairness	68%
Treatment with respect and dignity	65%
Being part of a team	54%
Company's interest in my well-being	52%

©Purdue University/BenchmarkPortal, Inc.

Figure 10. Elements of telephone agents that are important

34

Introduction

Contact centers by their very nature tend to de-personalize the CSRs' working environment. In a center, you typically find a large room full of standard working cubicles, which are a neutral, muted gray color. It is almost a "factory" look with production line employees. So the question is, "How can you individualize the CSR experience to make the job experience more personal?" In this chapter we will explore the following possibilities:

1. providing individual CSR recognition
2. effective listening to CSR issues
3. upward communications for CSRs
4. involving your CSRs in the decision-making process
5. providing clear and balanced expectations for CSRs.

Provide Individual Recognition

What's important to employees? The following table illustrates the gap that can exist when leaders don't ask their people what's important to them. It represents a ranking, by order of importance, of what employees *want* versus what managers *think* they want.[2]

Items ranked by employees and employers in order of important from 1 to 10 (1 is the highest) **What is important?**	Employee Perspective	Manager Perspective
(1) Appreciation	1	8
(2) Feeling "in" on things	2	10
(3) Help on personal problems	3	9

Table 4. What is important to employees?

This gap between what is *really* important to workers and what management *thinks* is important emphasizes how critical it is to *ask* directly what is most important to CSRs.

Here are some facts we found about CSRs within a customer contact center.

- The majority (over 80%) of a customer's impression of your company is based on the interaction they have with your CSRs.

- CSRs know firsthand what the primary issues are from the customer's perspective.

- CSRs are the internal "Voice of the Customer."

- CSRs, and supporting personnel, make up between 50% and 70% of the cost of running a customer contact center.

- An experienced CSR is able to provide better service than a new-hire CSR.

- Almost your entire brand image is in the hands (or, more specifically, the voice) of your CSRs.

These facts illustrate the depth of customer knowledge that exists with each CSR. Even if involving CSRs weren't an effective method of recognition, the best companies do seek their opinions and involvement simply based on the depth of their customer knowledge.

Here are four ways we have found to easily provide individual recognition to CSRs:

1. Listen to them often and intently.

2. Involve them wherever possible in planning and policy setting.

3. Appreciate what they do, and tell them often.

4. Recognize their contributions by a personalized reward system.

In the following paragraphs, we will address these four suggestions more specifically.

Listen to Your CSRs

Listen *carefully* to what your CSRs have to say. They are the front-line serving customers directly. Part of a retention champion's job is to listen and understand the issues of each person on the team. The CSRs know more than anyone about the issues that get in the way of providing exceptional service.

Listening contributes directly to the satisfaction level of each CSR as well. If a CSR doesn't feel listened to, or that his/her needs are not being met, the CSR's focus will turn inward. If, on the other hand, a CSR feels that the manager is focused on his/her happiness as an employee and person, they are free to focus directly on the customer.

So, whether a CSR needs to be heard regarding a customer issue, or a personal issue, the retention champion needs to actively listen. Once the situation is understood, the retention champion's role is to take action when needed by a) removing obstacles, b) providing additional support, c) solving problems, d) facilitating solutions, and e) just plain "running interference" for his/her people. Whatever it takes. But it starts by listening.

- Ask them what they need.
- After you ask, listen.
- Ask clarifying questions if needed.
- Then listen again.

Another level of listening involves soliciting improvement ideas. A retention champion is responsible for creating the environment that promotes active thinking and creative problem solving. If, however, there is not an effective system in place to evaluate and act on the ideas, the creative pool will quickly dry up.

One method is to set up effective *listening posts*. A listening post is a forum to collect information. Examples are regular opinion surveys or periodic employee satisfaction surveys.

One process that has a significant impact on the health of a call center environment is the **Upward Communication Process**. This process was introduced to us by Jack Callahan, who used it to deliver incredible results for Allstate Insurance. The process is intended to eliminate the "filter factor." A "filter factor" is the effect of having critical information "filtered" by

Educational Graffiti©

"Everything we learn about retention always leads us back to managers." Ross Schwab

37

each level within an organization as the information is relayed to each higher level of management. In other words, a supervisor may try to make everything seem smooth to his/her boss because s/he thinks if it's not, it is a direct reflection on his or her personal abilities. Then the manager relays even less to his/her manager and so on. The phrase we use is "The further up you go...the less you know."

The prime objective for the Upward Communication Process is to "get issues on the table" (so they can be addressed). There is no punitive aspect. Ideally, the person that is ultimately accountable for the results of the call center (usually the director or vice president) would conduct the meetings and be directly involved in making sure actions are taken. We will present a short summary of the process here.

Upward Communication Process

Each department/unit/team establishes a person to act as the team's spokesperson. We found that asking everyone on the team if they were interested and then putting all interested names in a hat and drawing one name for each quarter (three months) worked well.

The spokesperson for the team is provided with a short survey to give to their team members. The basic format is:

1. What's working?
2. What's not working?
3. What are we missing?

There's also a scale that quantifies how happy each member of the team is at that particular time, For example, on a 1 to 5 scale with 5 being "I enjoy coming to work almost everyday. I can't think of anything specific that I would change," to a 1 being, "I'm very unhappy in my role right now and I'm currently looking for another job."

The spokesperson would collect the anonymous surveys from the team and represent them at an "upward meeting."

Once a month, we met with the representatives from all the teams over a pizza lunch (we began by going to a local pizza shop, but then learned it was quieter and we could spend more time if we had pizza delivered). The meeting had a standard procedure:

1. Everyone introduces themselves, which area they represent, how long they have been with the company.

2. We establish a scribe and a timekeeper (so that everyone has their fair portion of time).

3. Randomly start with someone volunteering to go first (generally not someone there for the first time). They share the overall morale/atmosphere of their team and whether it was better or worse than the previous month. Then they share the top two to three issues from their team.

4. We take notes (but focus more on actively listening and understanding the issues). We ask clarifying questions and try to determine the core of the issue(s). Others generally jump in to support certain issues as being "big" this month. After an understanding is gained, we thank that person and move to the next person.

5. Continue around the table until everyone has had a chance to share.

6. Discuss with the entire team what we have heard (summarized). Ask for their help in determining which two to three issues overall should be the primary point of focus to resolve immediately.

7. We determine the top issues and they can go back and report that to their teams.

8. They can also give us the detailed surveys of team members if they feel there are unique issues that need to be addressed that didn't apply to everyone.

We found that there are some simple rules of engagement, namely:

1. It's not appropriate to talk about individuals in this setting. If there is a specific issue about a person, the spokesperson can meet with us in our office after the meeting.

Educational Graffiti©

"The best index to a person's character is how he treats people who can't do him any good, and how he treats people who can't fight back." Abigail Van Buren

2. Balance the positive and negative (thus the "what's working" section).

3. Always look for the solution and don't just present the "problems."

The biggest key to making this process work is to take ACTION on the issues raised in the meeting. By seeing results to sharing their perspective, the team members feel that they are being heard and are able to make a difference.

Initially, the middle managers felt at risk when this process began. They thought it would be a negative reflection on them if there were issues. We shared that the primary reason for these meetings is to make sure all important issues got on the table. We need to know what they are to be able to address them. It was rare that there were issues related to a single manager. The managers were much more excited about the process when we added a step of "debriefing" with them after the meeting. They could then be "in the know" about what was discussed and could be part of the solutions immediately. It also helped because sometimes the spokespeople would update the rest of the team before the manager even knew what issues were discussed.

Involve Your CSRs

It's important to find effective methods of tapping into the wealth of CSR knowledge and take CSR ideas and improvement suggestions seriously and most importantly to take action on these great ideas. By nature, CSRs tend to be friendly problem-solvers who take pride in making people happy. These same traits sometimes work against them when they need to pound their fist on a table to fight for changes, for themselves or for the customer. Many times, because most CSRs don't especially enjoy "conflict," if an issue isn't resolved, they will simply remove themselves, physically from the situation (i.e., they will quit), and we will lose an excellent CSR because of management inaction.

Retention champions understand these factors and find "non-confrontational" ways to solicit CSR ideas and suggestions.

We suggest that you seek their input on improvement ideas. Act on as many of the suggestions as possible. Give them credit. Communicate back to them on progress.

CSRs that are engaged are less likely to leave. To create a level of engagement (or commitment), it is important to include CSRs in information sharing beyond a "need to know" level. They need to feel that they are in the loop and not the last to know. They need to feel like there is a level of trust by sharing overall organization concerns. It promotes a feeling of everyone being together whether or not the news is good.

The Donnelly Corporation,[20] for example, opens communications by placing huge posters throughout their customer contact center with ten questions for all employees to ask each other about. They list such questions as:

"What took too long today?"
"What requires too many sign-offs?"
"What is just plain silly?"

And yet, we know from our research into turnover, many of these great interactions seldom happen. Because there is almost always an urgency to make sure the phones are covered, very little time is spent soliciting the thoughts, insights and ideas from the most customer-knowledgeable employees we have, namely the CSRs.

A Best Practice Case Study

USAA launched its ECHO Program (Every Contact Has Opportunities). Each customer contact has the potential of producing improvement suggestions. To capitalize on this, USAA developed their program called ECHO. Comments from customers, including complaints, compliments or suggestions for a new product or service are logged immediately into a tracking system. The comments are then transferred immediately to a team of Action Agents, who are responsible for acting on the referrals. Weekly analysis of the changes and suggestions made are circulated from the front-line employees to the top management. USAA logs thousands of entries per week into their ECHO Program and it works marvelously well.

Educational Graffiti©

"The key element in good business management is emotional attitude. The rest is mechanics." Harvey Geenan

Appreciate What Your CSRs Do

Appreciation is an emotional need or state of mind. It's a feeling of gratitude and of belonging and of being needed. The key to successful appreciation is to express it when you experience it, and to experience it often. The need to appreciate others will grow when you develop the axiom of "Having an Attitude of Gratitude."

Another key is to be sincere. Insincerity creates more damage than if no appreciation was attempted at all. Rather than apply a generic "line" when someone does something worthy of recognition, try an approach described as the "double-layer compliment." Here's how it works:

- Get the person's attention.

- Compliment the overall action (example: "You really did a great job with Ms. Jones today"). This is the first layer.

- Tell the person one or two *specific* things that stood out (example: "I was really impressed with how creative you were in getting the check delivered today. You really seem to have a special ability to take a complex situation and make it appear easy to solve.")

- Then, depending on the relationship (and if the feeling is sincere), you could close with a comment like, "I feel very fortunate to have you on my team."

Another way to look at this method is to think of compliments as something being applied to the skin (like various lotions). A generic compliment is very topical. It doesn't last long. By using the double-layer compliment approach, its like applying something to the skin that is absorbed into the system. It can have a long-lasting effect and can even provide positive side effects.

It is also important to provide acknowledgements frequently. One method to help increase the number of times appreciation is expressed is to create a cross-log listing of all the names on your team with spaces next to each name. Each time a sincere compliment or expression of appreciation is given, simply place a checkmark next to that person's name. Have a goal in mind. It will help keep the focus at the top of your mind, and track progress as you develop this critical skill of a retention champion.

One manager developed a unique approach. To remind himself to acknowledge his team every day, he places ten paper clips in his left-hand pocket each morning. Each time he praises a staff member, he moves a paper clip to the right-hand pocket. His goal is to make sure all ten paper clips get moved to the right-hand pocket each day.[16]

A man in a pay phone booth at a restaurant was overheard by the restaurant manager completing a telephone call.

"Hello, Mr. Smith?" he was heard to say. "I understand you have been looking for an assistant." He paused to listen to the response. "Oh, you hired one two months ago and are pleased with your choice? Well, thank you anyway. I hope you continue to be satisfied with your decision."

When he hung up the phone, the restaurant manager commented, "I happened to overhear your conversation. I'm sorry you didn't get a shot at that job."

"Oh, that's all right," the man replied, "That was my boss. I was hired as his assistant three months ago and I was just phoning to find out how I'm doing!"

Employees like to know how they're doing. When was the last time that you as a manager gave them some positive feedback?

Do you wait until they ask or contact you?

Recognize the CSR's Contributions

Many reward and recognition programs apply a blanket program and assume it will work for all. That's like assuming that we would all choose the same dessert as our favorite. Just as each person brings their history and life experiences with them, each person has their own preference on how they prefer to be recognized and rewarded.

Educational Graffiti©

"I guess our greatest technique and our greatest accomplishment is this commitment to communicating with them (Wal-Mart employees) in every way that we possibly can, and listening to them constantly. You've got to put their interest first, and eventually it will come back to the company." Sam Walton

Here are some examples to use when asking your employees what matters most to them:[27]

Forms of recognition

- an award, preferably given in front of my peers
- a plaque to hang on my wall
- a thank you, in writing, from my boss
- a note to my boss's boss about my excellent performance
- frequent pats on the back
- my boss actually implementing one of my ideas
- a chance to be on a really exciting, cutting edge project
- a bonus of some sort
- a day off
- words of praise in front of my family
- a raise
- a chance to go to lunch with senior management
- opportunity to work with people from other parts of the company
- a promotion
- a change in my title
- a small memento or gift
- some flexibility in my schedule.

Here are some general guidelines for effective recognition:[23]

Spontaneity. Catch them doing something right and thank them then and there.

Specifically. Praise their efforts for *specific* (rather than generic) accomplishments or efforts. Sometimes referred to as a "double-layer" compliment (tell them generally what you appreciate; then tell them what they did *specifically* that made you appreciate it).

Purposefully. Take an employee out to lunch or dinner at a great restaurant to show your appreciation of work well done. A variation on this theme is treat your employee and their guest to dinner at a great restaurant and pick up the bill.

Privately. Go to your employee's cubical or office to give a personal thank you and praise.

Publicly. Praise an employee in the presence of others (peers, your boss, family members).

In writing. Send a letter, memo or e-mail. Possibly send a copy to team members or higher-level management. Include a copy in their permanent human resource file. Mail a copy of your appreciation letter home to their spouse as a nice surprise.

Just-In-Time Recognition Program

One contact center developed an effective just-in-time (JIT) spot method of rewarding CSRs. Because many "spot" award programs are subject to the diligence of the individual manager (and how willing they are to shop/buy gift certificates, etc., on their own time), the JIT program solved that issue. Here's how it worked:

- The entire team was surveyed to determine the types of rewards that were the most valued.

- A supply of those rewards were purchased and stocked.

- A single person (in this case, a secretary) maintained the inventory.

- Managers simply had to select the reward (based on the CSRs' personal preferences) from the stock and sign a form to indicate who was being rewarded and why.

- A cross-check report was generated once a month to ensure that every manager was using the program and providing appropriate rewards.

A case study of customized recognition

Well known for its ability to retain great employees, State Farm Insurance uses a simple approach to the mass customization of employee recognition. Managers ask their employees to complete a one-page "Favorites List" of such things as their favorite ice cream, color, flower, movie star, candy bar, restaurant, food, vacation getaway spot, hobby, recreational activity--you get the point. When managers want to reward an employee for outstanding performance, they review that employee's "Favorites List" and quickly customize the recognition to include the individual employee's favorite things.[8]

In addition to understanding each team-member's preferred recognition method, it's also important to make sure that the recognition method is delivered sincerely. As described below, when a method seems less than sincere, the effect is lost.

Presentation is Everything

An effective award presentation makes a significant impression.[17]

- 97% of employees felt their "contribution was acknowledged" after an "excellent" award presentation.

- 39% of employees felt their "contribution was acknowledged" after a "poor" award presentation.

- 93% of employees felt an "excellent" award presentation "built commitment."

- 41% of employees felt stronger commitment to their organization after a "poor" award presentation.

Verbatim comments from in-service practitioners in the Purdue Study:

"Treat the phone representatives as the most important part of your organization - they are."

"We also did skip-level (supervisors were skipped) meetings once a month. This was a meeting with the representatives to share information. We also created an Advisory Committee that helped our management solve the tough issues."

"If representatives are happy in their position and acknowledged for their accomplishments, they rarely look for other opportunities much less leave for other positions. Our initiative is an ongoing one to address morale issues and acknowledge/reward individual performance. Some of the components are an employee of the month award, ongoing and instant recognition for customer commendations, "early-leave" points awarded to representatives caught in the act of delighting our customers, and 15 minutes of our monthly meeting devoted to kudos."

"Employee recognition and expressed sincere appreciation from the management level will help to greatly reduce turnover. Another excellent method is to get to know the employee and understand what "language" they speak. Some want words of affirmation while others want gifts or one-on-one time with the manager. Knowing which "language" applies to a particular employee and utilizing the appropriate "language" agent by agent will reap significant results."

"Include CSRs in planning and implementation of service/contact center initiatives."

"Make each agent feel important and that they make a difference."

Educational Graffiti©

"Your job gives you authority. Your behavior gives you respect." Irwin Federman

Provide Clear and Balanced Expectations

What are balanced expectations? We found that many managers we interviewed are struggling with the answer to the age-old contact center question: "What's more important...the quality of a single call, or the quantity of calls handled?"

In most cases, the answer is both. While exceptional service should always be the primary goal (taking whatever time is needed), it is also important to know that the CSR is in control of the contact and is efficient in the way that that contact is handled. We have developed a balanced score-card approach to quality (effectiveness) and quantity (efficiency). This formula can be found on our Web site at BenchmarkPortal.com.

Defining the balanced expectations is a challenge. The quantity measures are the easy part. For example, performance on average delay, abandoned rates and average talk time are reported directly from the telephone system and switch. They are reflections of the level of telephone service and are important to be at or close to best practice standards. These numbers are understood easily by everyone. Unfortunately for many customer contact centers, these numbers by themselves are often exceptional even with extremely poor service.

The tougher, and more important, numbers to capture and report are the soft numbers:

- the customer satisfaction rating
- the employee satisfaction levels
- the quality of the contact.

These are the measures that are important in defining the success of the customer contact center. Most contact centers don't have effective methods in place to routinely capture these measures. Even when they do collect some data, there is confusion about how the numbers should be interpreted.

Consider having CSRs as part of a cross-section team to develop the performance metrics for the department. While there are some general measures that every contact center captures, the actual performance level and ranges may be open for discussion. By having direct involvement, you will end up with measures that not only feel "fair" to the CSRs, but the team will feel more ownership of the measures because they were involved in defining them.

How to make the goals or expectations clear for all concerned

Management strategies, such as "management by objective" and "balanced scorecard" and "total quality management," all focus on harnessing CSR performance. In a way, all these strategies recognize the role of goal-directed behavior and the value of the front-line worker in driving business profitability. Simply stated, an individual will engage in behavior that will lead to the attainment of goals for rewards valued by that individual.

Expectations need to be clear and documented to be credible. Within the contact center environment, some metrics are more reasonable when given in ranges, and knowing exactly what the range is provides a clear target. Another rule of thumb is to keep the number of expectations to a minimum, but make sure you're measuring the metrics that are directly tied to caller satisfaction, such as percentage of calls resolved on first contact. From research conducted at Purdue and sponsored by IBM, "first time final" (also known as "once and done") calls are the highest caller satisfaction driver (see figure 11).

Educational Graffiti©

"Leadership is not rank, privileges, titles, or money. It is responsibility." Peter Drucker

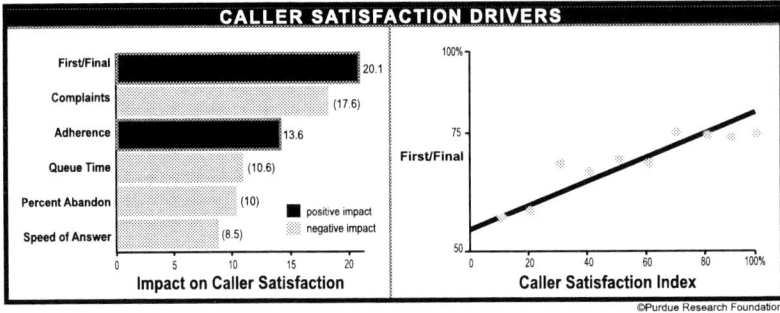

CALLER SATISFACTION DRIVERS

First/Final	20.1
Complaints	(17.6)
Adherence	13.6
Queue Time	(10.6)
Percent Abandon	(10)
Speed of Answer	(8.5)

■ positive impact
▨ negative impact

Impact on Caller Satisfaction

First/Final

Caller Satisfaction Index

©Purdue Research Foundation

Figure 11. Above we have plotted call center performance metrics that have a statistically significant impact on caller satisfaction. The strongest correlation comes from First / Final, which is the percentage of issues that are resolved on the first call without any transfers or calls back. Since First / Final was the strongest driver of caller satisfaction, we drilled down on the data and found that there is an almost linear relationship between First / Final and agent turnover. Simply stated, inexperienced new agents are less able to complete an issue on the first call, and consequently are less able to satisfy callers.

Also, the more CSR-specific expectations are, the more motivating they are. For example:

There are tools today that provide CSRs with feedback about how satisfied *their* particular callers were with the service *they* personally provided. Because, while it's easy to assess whether the information provided was technically accurate and the procedures were followed in detail, the real test is whether or not the caller was satisfied, or delighted, with the service provided. By using an online, immediately after-contact survey, CSRs receive real-time feedback about the service that was *just* provided.

Great feedback and ways to ensure success

There are several factors that determine whether a feedback system is effective. First, does it produce the desired result? Does the CSR feel motivated to either continue (doing well) or to improve where needed? The second factor is about the "when" and "how" of the feedback. Is it timely? Is it shared in a constructive, positive tone? And, finally, when performance is not where it

50

should be, is the person who is providing the feedback also comfortable addressing awkward or uncomfortable situations?

CSRs need tangible information to increase their motivation and satisfaction level, highlighted by clear and purposeful activities linked to reward and recognition.

Consistent, accurate feedback is critical. In a busy contact center, meeting with each CSR on a regular basis can be a challenge. There are two approaches that can help make the feedback more successful:

- Review results with each CSR on a pre-scheduled basis (NOT to be moved or cancelled). These meetings have to be considered critical.

- Provide as much performance detail automatically to CSRs as possible. One of the latest developments in CSR management is to provide real-time performance feedback to each CSR throughout the day, directly to their own PC.

Warning: CSRs quickly learn how to "work" the numbers!

When we had our first customer service team, we were striving for record-breaking performance. One afternoon, toward the end of the day, we noticed that one CSR was handling several contacts very quickly. As we approached her, she and another CSR started giggling. We asked what was going on and they said they were just "contributing to our performance." They had figured out that by contacting an outside line and dialing our customer service number that all they had to do was answer the contacts and it improved the abandoned rate, the average speed of answer *and* the average talk time.

Educational Graffiti©

"Leadership is not the private reserve of a few charismatic men and women. It is a process ordinary managers use when they are bringing forth the best from themselves and others." Anonymous

A retention champion makes sure that:

- everyone knows what is expected
- everyone knows that his/her personal contribution fits into the bigger scheme of things
- everyone receives timely, honest feedback in a constructive atmosphere.

Everyone wants to feel important, but what makes one person **feel** acknowledged and appreciated can be very different from the next person. The key is in understanding each team member's preferences.

A retention champion needs to know each person's preferences in areas such as how they prefer to be recognized (publicly or privately) and what each person feels is a real "reward" (time off, special privileges, off-the-phone time, flexible shifts, education options, and many more).

Before we move on, let's once again try to understand the extent of the challenge of the turnover problem. In a recent poll of over 1,000 contact center managers, we found the results depicted in figure 12. From these results, we estimate that the average turnover reported was approximately 19%.

If we study our complete database of over 5,000 contact centers, the average for all industries is 28%. From our industry estimates, there are approximately 3,000,000 CSRs working in the roughly 200,000 contact centers in North America. Even at a 20% turnover level, this amounts to approximately 600,000 new CSRs that must be recruited and trained each year.

Verbatim comments from in-service practitioners in the Purdue Study:

"Implementing a caller satisfaction incentive bonus plan, allowing for increasing bonuses year after year, based on customer satisfaction achievement levels. Based on customer satisfaction performance, an employee can earn $5K after one year, $10K after 2 years, $15K after 3 years and $20K after four years.

"Performance is rewarded against corporate customer satisfaction goals, but the stepped-up bonus amounts have inherent retention incentive. Costs are justified by reduced cost of turnover, productivity gains of having more experienced agents, and long-term profitability of the corporation through improved customer satisfaction and loyalty. This plan has reduced turnover from 31% to 17%."

"In three separate instances I've seen agent turnover rates dropping by 7%, 10% and 8% after introduction of formal contact quality processes. This is more than coincidence."

"Introducing proactive agent contact quality monitoring and coaching. This had the effect of markedly improving the ability of agents to effectively handle contacts through to a successful resolution (including a happy customer) creating greater job satisfaction and reduced stress levels. Of course, the other major benefit was the happy customers. A win all round."

"Introduction of the SITEL Management System (SMS) which enabled us to share agent performance data in a real-time basis, twice a day."

"Providing people with clear, objective performance expectations, reporting and tracking of actual performance to those expectations, reviewing with the individual the progress against those expectations."

"Our turnover was caused by a hopelessly static CSR performance management system. People frequently were rewarded for the wrong results, at the wrong time, and with the wrong reward."

Educational Graffiti©
"People don't quit organizations…people quit people." Anonymous

Literature Search Findings on Individual Recognition and Incentives

The Reverend Dr. Martin Luther King said, "If you want to move people, it has to be toward a vision that's positive for them, that taps important values, that gets them something they desire, and it has to be presented in a compelling way that they feel inspired to follow." This is the challenge for contact center leadership.

In a survey conducted by the University of Maryland, employees were asked to rank the ten things they wanted most in the workplace. Appreciation was ranked number one. Benefits ranked third.[16]

Literature Search Findings on Best Practices in Telephone Service

Customer service performance determines worker incentives. Numerous recognition and reward incentives (over 45 such approaches at one world-class organization) help to recognize and reinforce desirable work behavior and noteworthy job performance. Front-line workers play a leading role in the development of performance appraisal and recognition systems at world-class organizations.[14]

What level of total annual turnover do you experience at your call center?

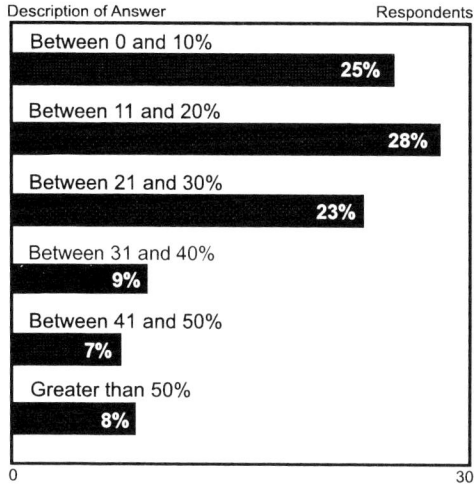

Description of Answer	Respondents
Between 0 and 10%	25%
Between 11 and 20%	28%
Between 21 and 30%	23%
Between 31 and 40%	9%
Between 41 and 50%	7%
Greater than 50%	8%

0   30

Figure 12. This bar chart shows the answers to our question, "What level of total annual turnover do you experience in your call center?"

Literature Search Findings on Clear and Balanced Exceptions

We found survey information that indicated 65% of CSRs that left the contact center felt they did not receive coaching or feedback for career growth. Incumbent CSRs at the same center didn't feel informed of the center goals or their performance in achieving those goals.[8]

Literature Search Findings on Best Practices for Telephone Service

Job standards for front-line workers and managers alike should reflect a commitment to delighting the customer. Furthermore, job standards should be tied to key customer "satisfiers," and should clearly communicate the extent to which front-line CSRs are empowered to serve customers. Mixed messages must be avoided (e.g., front-line workers are told to

Educational Graffiti©
"The deepest principle of human nature is a craving to be appreciated." William James

take the time needed to satisfy callers, and hence, are not directly evaluated on the average length of the contacts they handle). Performance expectations may be documented through a written contract between the team leader and the front-line CSR. The contract identifies yearly goals and outlines a course of action the worker intends to take to meet those goals. This process encourages front-line CSRs to buy-in to the overarching organizational goals and objectives.[14]

Here is a best practice example from Serving the American Public.

1. Each front-line worker typically interacts with some 25,000 customers per year. An integral part of the continuous improvement process is the free flow of ideas from these key customer-contact personnel.

2. World-class contact center operations typically implement over five suggestions per employee per year.

3. Managers at successful contact center operations actively solicit front-line workers' advice on how to improve processes at biweekly team meetings, and periodically give the suggestion program added emphasis through recurring suggestion contests and specific promotional campaigns.

4. Online suggestion systems facilitate the submission of ideas. With online systems, suggestion receipt is immediately acknowledged.

5. Those making suggestions are notified within 24 hours as to who is evaluating their ideas, and receive additional feedback as to the status of their idea on at least a weekly basis.

6. In world-class operations, nearly all suggestions are completely processed within 72 hours.

Purdue University Research Findings

According to Purdue Benchmark Research, team leader "coaches" typically monitor five to ten calls for each front-line CSR each month. A primary purpose of the observation is to identify individual training needs as part of an organization-wide continuous improvement effort. Since the emphasis is on constructive suggestions for improving customer service, observations are not necessarily tied to the performance assessment process. Frequent, regular reports based on information gathered from service observation of telephone contacts (sometimes called, "Quality Tips")[20] are distributed to all front-line CSRs. Front-line workers receive immediate feedback on ways to improve their contact-handling skills, and immediate recognition if superior service has been provided to a caller. Both silent/remote and side-by-side monitoring are used.

In preparation for writing this book we asked contact center human resource managers how they measure the performance of the CSRs. Figure 13 shows that quality monitoring scores are at the top, followed closely by attendance, and then adherence to schedule.

How do you measure the performance of your telephone agents?

Answer

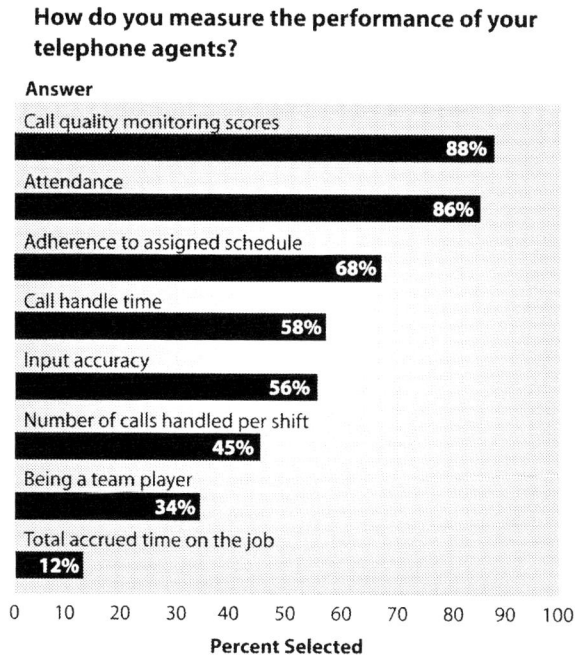

Figure 13. This bar chart shows the answers to our question, "How do you measure the performance of your telephone agents?" The top three are quality monitoring, attendance, and adherence.

Educational Graffiti©
"Every little quit hurts." Anonymous

Continuous Investment in CSR Development

There are many benefits to "investing" in CSRs. First, by increasing their knowledge, they are able to serve callers with more confidence and are better able to resolve issues on first contact (the strongest caller satisfaction driver). They are also able to make informed judgments in complex cases and thereby act on their own to problem solve with callers.

Properly trained and re-trained CSRs are more satisfied because they feel that the company cares about them, professionally and personally. The level of professionalism increases when the energy is focused on proactive growth and learning. Many managers we spoke to are considering CSR certification as another investment in professionals. For those readers interested, Purdue offers a certification program at the CSR, supervisor, and manager levels through its College of Call Center Excellence (additional information is at our Web site, BenchmarkPortal.com).

Furthermore, as we study our database, it also becomes clear that the length of training has a major impact on minimizing CSR turnover. In figure 14, contact centers with "extensive" training, and re-training, have less than half the turnover as compared to centers with less training.

Length of Initial Agent Training

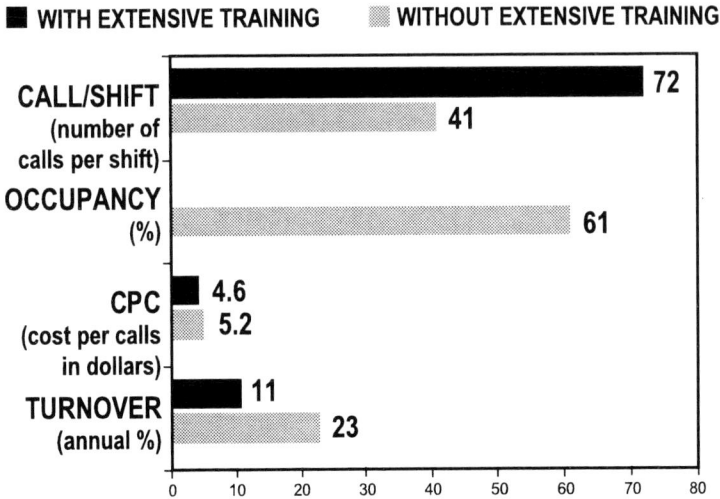

■ **WITH EXTENSIVE TRAINING**   ▓ **WITHOUT EXTENSIVE TRAINING**

CALL/SHIFT (number of calls per shift) — 72 / 41

OCCUPANCY (%) — 61

CPC (cost per calls in dollars) — 4.6 / 5.2

TURNOVER (annual %) — 11 / 23

Figure 14. From this chart, we can see that agents who undergo extensive initial training (including CBT, classroom and side-by-side training) are more than twice as likely to stay in the contact center.

High-value CSRs typically have an extensive skill set. They have:

- the ability to effectively multi-task
- incredible attention to detail
- superior skills at working with all kinds of people
- excellent verbal and written skills
- to constantly absorb new and changing information
- to think quickly on their feet
- to be detectives and effective problem solvers
- superior diplomacy skills.

As skilled and intelligent as CSRs are in their profession, they, like anyone else, don't want to stagnate in their career growth. They want to continue to learn new things. In the contact center environment, special attention needs to be spent on making sure each CSR is given the opportunity to learn and grow. Without this, CSRs, especially the talented ones, will become frustrated and leave (i.e., dysfunctional turnover). These

CSRs are exactly the ones you want to keep, and from our experience, they are quite "savable" with the proper retention strategies in place.

The retention champion understands this, of course. With each CSR, the manager will probe to determine where each CSR's interest in learning lies. In some cases, it may be to become cross-trained in all areas of customer service to provide one-stop-shopping for the customer. For another, they may be interested in marketing, and the learning may come in the form of company-supported college classes.

The retention champion must build time into the staffing and scheduling models to allow for training and continuing education. It cannot be a second-hand thought. It has to be a conscious decision and a long-term commitment.

Luckily, there are technologies and solutions that make it easier to address this issue today. First, with an effective forecasting and scheduling system, CSRs can be scheduled for supplemental training without creating an impact to the service levels. This is assuming that your staffing levels support CSR development.

Second, there are products that provide flexibility in offering supplemental training even at the desktop. This solution works especially well in contact centers where there are peaks and valleys in call volumes. By adhering to a close coordination with the scheduling system, CSRs are able to learn in bite-size pieces throughout the day.

Training Through Simulation

One of the most effective ways to reduce contact center turnover is to improve the training that agents receive, both before they are introduced to a live environment and once they have become experienced agents. Until recently, the strategies primarily used were traditional instructor-led training, role-playing, and computer-based training modules. While effective when used as knowledge transfer tools, these methods are unable

---

Educational Graffiti©

"Be faithful to your job and co-workers by being on time, starting promptly, and doing your share of the work. Treat others with respect, both as human beings and co-workers. Refrain from bickering, gossip and horseplay." USAA Code of Conduct

to provide the most critical element for preparing agents to interact with customers—real-life experience in the safety of the training environment.

In recent years, however, new technology has emerged that is dramatically improving the training that contact centers are able to deliver. Known as simulation, this technology is allowing contact centers to expose agents in training to customer calls exactly as they would occur on the floor.

Simulation is a broadly used term and one that has many definitions. It is used to describe everything from computer-based training to on-line learning. However, the best results to date have been achieved through simulation technology capable of integrating both voice and data to simulate real-life, on-the-job conditions.

The technology works by replicating calls exactly as they occur in a live contact center, providing true to life training simulations. Students listen to customers, respond to them verbally, and navigate through applications exactly as they would in a live call. What they see, hear, and do is no different from a real customer interaction. Some applications allow students to take a building block approach to learning, giving them the ability to practice different elements of a call separately and view "ideal" call scenarios. Instructors can also incorporate coaching into simulations to correct trainees as they practice and include other communication vehicles, such as web chat and email, in the training process.

The benefits of this approach are tied directly to skill and confidence building. Because agents are able to experience a live environment and make mistakes safely, they know what to expect and develop confidence in their ability to be successful (see figure 15).

Use of Computer-Based Training

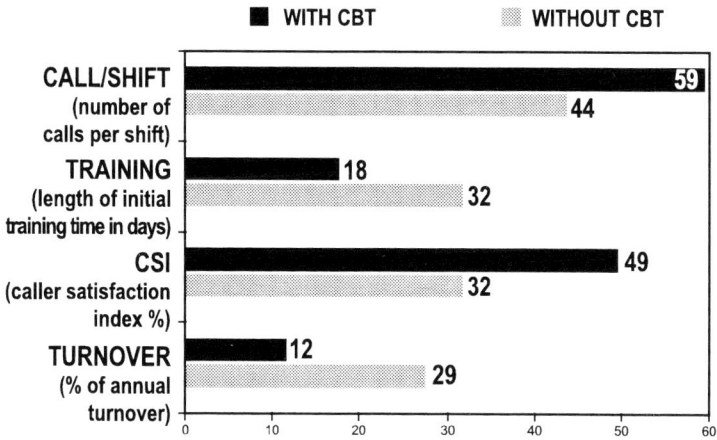

■ WITH CBT   ▒ WITHOUT CBT

CALL/SHIFT (number of calls per shift)	59 / 44
TRAINING (length of initial training time in days)	18 / 32
CSI (caller satisfaction index %)	49 / 32
TURNOVER (% of annual turnover)	12 / 29

Figure 15. From this chart, we can see that companies that use some form of CBT are rewarded with an overall turnover rate that is less than half of that of companies without CBT.

Although relatively new, simulation technology is growing in popularity because of the results companies are able to achieve. To date, the most significant benefits are being realized in the areas of turnover and productivity. Contact centers are finding that agents who have been trained using simulation are less likely to become frustrated on the job and generally more satisfied with their work environments. Looking at productivity, agents are achieving call handle time goals more quickly and have lower error rates. In one study conducted by a Fortune 500 hospitality chain, results showed that attrition was 33% lower and call time more than 20 seconds shorter for agents trained using simulation technology versus their traditional approach.

For more information and a case study on simulation, training and details on the study mentioned above, refer to page 155.

Educational Graffiti©

"I tried to create an environment where they were encouraged to be more of who they already were." Anonymous

Verbatim comments from in-service practitioners in the Purdue Study:

"The most compelling solution to agent turnover was that of a unique offering of employee benefits coupled with education reimbursements. They also offered an education reimbursement package with limits per year for complete reimbursement for the employee's college education. The yearly limit on the expenditure allowed the employees to complete their college degree within a six- year period, knowing that if they left the company, they would have to pay on their own, kept the employee there for at least six years."

"Cross-training! It made the agents more productive as they could handle more contacts. It made their jobs more interesting as they handled a greater variety of contacts. They tend to stay longer because they are not in a dead-end position. I am able to justify increases because of their total added value to the company."

"We encouraged job rotation so employees could experience different customer and technical environments. This required setting the right customer expectations as well as marketing the benefit for both the employee and the customer."

"We have implemented a new extended training program that has three modules. This gives the employee time to acclimate to the surroundings and have time to concentrate on smaller bits of information at a time. We also have developed training to promote our clients and all the good they do. The employees like this because they feel good about what they are doing."

Create a Bonding Environment

From the time a CSR begins orientation and training, they are self-assessing whether or not they will fit into the existing environment. In this book, we define a "retention champion" as a manager that is well versed in all the important CSR handling skills discussed in our book, and one that really understands that they are the number one reason that CSRs stay or leave the organization. There are several things a "retention champion" can do to help new CSRs assimilate into their new world. Here are some examples:

1. **Give trainees the basics.** Make sure all the new hires know the "what, where, who, when and why" of the area they will eventually join.

2. **Establish early ties with current team members.** Assign successful existing CSRs to eat lunch with them to answer questions (and make them feel more comfortable).

3. **Help classmates bond.** The trainers can do some icebreakers with the new hires classes to help develop bonding of classmates. One company had trainees who were just released from class do a scavenger hunt and find out different things about the environment (as a team) to help them get comfortable. Some of the items they had to find were a) Who organizes the birthday celebrations? b) Where does outgoing mail go? c) Which manager used to be a professional ballerina?

4. **Handhold during transition period.** Once the class is formally released, rather than having the trainees disperse and fend for themselves (with a possible cube "buddy"), create some sort of transition space for them. One example is a Training Hub (or Nesting Area) with desks on the working floor, but with more handholding as the trainees began to take more live contacts. This approach helps the trainees feel more competent and confident and provides a safe environment to ask questions and fill in the training gaps.

5. **Let trainees have some say.** Once the trainees are comfortable (based on being able to handle certain contacts/volumes accurately and independently), they will join the existing team with less anxiety. When possible, let the transition date be trainee-driven.

Educational Graffiti©

"There's no reason that work has to be suffused with seriousness.... Professionalism can be worn lightly. Fun is a stimulant to people. They enjoy their work more and work more productively." Herb Kelleher

A Feeling of Belonging

CSRs that don't feel like they belong will generally not participate in any team-building or fun or social activities. They don't sign up for baseball teams, don't engage in "cube decorating contests" and don't participate in Secret Santa around the Christmas Holidays.

"It's like a family." That's the comment we heard over and over again from long-term CSRs. Especially in a customer contact center, there are several parallels to the home/family and work/employee environments. You spend the bulk of your time with other people. You can't choose your family nor can you choose your co-workers. In both the home and at work, you want to feel like everyone truly cares about you and would be there for you if you really needed help. In either the home or at work, you don't always get along with everyone all the time, but over time, most things work themselves out. And, in both situations, you weather the tough times and the good times together. This is a bonding experience.

Retention champions look for these signs and try to find ways to engage those CSRs. While there is always room for individualism and those that don't particularly like group activities, the manager needs to make sure that the "arms-length" behavior is being done for the right reasons (not because they feel like an outsider).

Some ways of engaging CSRs that feel outside the group are:

- Have them get involved in some solution-sessions with other CSRs
- Ask them to be accountable for some specific assignment (such as being the special contact for a key business account)
- Ask others for help. When it is an option, the manager can recruit the help of a trusted informal leader on the team (a team lead or technical specialist). That person may be more involved in the day-to-day activities and may be able to provide insight as to behavior that is contributing to the CSR's being excluded (or being self-excluding).

The bottom line is that when a CSR doesn't feel like they belong, they won't stay with the company for long. It's too painful for them.

The All Important "Fun Factor"

Assuming that everyone does get along with each other, and that they feel like part of the "work family," having an atmosphere that is light and supportive can be a huge aspect of retaining CSRs. When people enjoy coming to work because they know they are valued, and they genuinely enjoy most of the people they work with, they don't even *think* about what other options they might have.

A contact center is an environment unlike any other. Physically, it is a tightly placed team (e.g., physical environment) that is usually open to all. A contact center is a "company within a company." There isn't much privacy. It is almost always busy. There is almost always a "crisis of the day," and everyone is dealing with people, both on the team and with calling customers. Although stress comes with the territory in a customer service contact center, a caring environment can go a long way in minimizing some of the natural stress of the job.

CSRs seem to love to celebrate. We found that most contact centers have a monthly birthday lunch and routinely have potluck meals where everyone brings something to share. There are baby showers, wedding showers, going-away parties, Halloween parties, and many more. It all adds to the "work family" effect, and from our experience, you should encourage this atmosphere to minimize turnover.

The retention champion not only promotes the routine celebrations, but also looks for other opportunities to "mix it up." One formal period is during Customer Service Week in early October. Some of the best contact centers get very creative in the ways they celebrate. Some examples are a) valet parking for CSRs for the day, b) washing CSRs' cars, c) giving CSRs breaks

---

Educational Graffiti©

"Keep away from people who try to belittle your ambitions. Small people always do that, but the really great make you feel that you, too, can become great." Mark Twain

by covering the phone for them, d) offering on-site massages, and finally e) conducting raffles and drawings for special prizes purchased by the center.

Informal Leader Effect

Along with the "retention champion," the "informal leaders" can make or break the contact center culture. They can either be in "leadership type" roles (like team leads) or they can simply be team members and have an influential role on the team. They are the ones that CSRs talk to when they need to confide or vent and are sought out by CSR for their opinions whenever changes are occurring. The retention champion knows to engage the informal leaders and to ask for their help during rough periods.

Case study of a company that makes it fun.

During a presentation at the Call Center Campus Conference at Purdue University, Kathy Woods described that Southwest Airlines is famous for its fun culture, and more importantly for this book, has less than 2% turnover rate of their front-line personnel. They operate with a leadership approach entitled:

"Managing from the Heart"

The basic principles are:

- Treat others as you want to be treated.
- Encourage your employees to be themselves and show their personalities.
- Be accessible. Have an open door policy.
- Be visible. Talk with your employees often.
- Be compassionate. Have empathy.
- Meet employees halfway. Give them B.O.D. (benefit of the doubt).

> **Verbatim comments from in-service practitioners in the Purdue Study:**
>
> "It's not all about pay - it's about creating an environment where the employee feels valued and part of a community."
>
> "We have trouble attracting employees because we are not convenient to public transportation. However, those employees who stay with us, do so because of the work environment. We offer a casual work place, flexible schedules and consistent non-dollar rewards. Several employees have moved from retail stores to our contact center and stress that the set schedules and relaxed atmosphere make them happy to come to work."
>
> "The ability to recognize agents' accomplishments combined with building a family environment."
>
> "Being accepted by the long time guys."

Providing Opportunities for Advancement

Most CSRs want some acknowledgement of their increased value to the company. To reduce turnover, there needs to be visible advancement track and a career path for CSRs.

There are two primary tracks to consider for advancement. First, to create advancement opportunities within the contact center through a defined career path. Second, to help develop and position CSRs for promotions within the organization.

Career Path Advancement

The most common advancement opportunities in the contact center are tiered positions within the department. Because most contact centers handle a variety of inquiries, it is generally fairly easy to create promotional positions, i.e., Level One, Level Two, Level Three, and more. Skill-based routing of telephone calls also lends itself to defining proficiency levels for CSRs, namely, the software routes the call to the CSR most proficient in handling this type of caller.

Educational Graffiti©

"For a manager to be perceived as a positive manager, they need a four to one positive to negative contact ratio." Kenneth Blanchard

Here is a career path example. When CSRs are released from class, they are considered a trainee. Once they have demonstrated a threshold level of competence (in both quality and quantity), they are promoted to a Level One CSR role (from our visits to many contact centers, advancement titles differ by company, but the concept is the same). Generally, if the CSR has learned additional functions or become extremely proficient in a single function (as a mentor might be), there may be an additional promotion to a Level II CSR role. These levels are generally available to all CSRs.

Most contact centers also have a certain number of senior level CSRs positions. Some center managers may define these as mentors, or as a Level III CSR. Others may consider "team leads" (which usually are accountable for some first line leadership functions) as Level III. Some may consider CSRs that handle the highest profile or complicated cases a Level III role. Regardless of what is included in the role, knowing that there are several career positions available for advancement, even if some require formal applications and testing, helps retain talented CSRs.

In addition, we found that a single contact center may have functionally different CSR jobs, allowing another avenue for career advancement within the center. A typical breakdown of call center functionality might be CSRs handling pre-sales questions, versus those handling order taking and tracking, versus those handling technical support. In figure 16 we show how these functions differ in turnover potential.

Performance Metrics

Call Center Functions	Cost per Call (dollars)	Annual Turnover (percent)	Caller Satisfaction Index (percent)	Average After Call Work Time (minutes)	Average Queue Time (seconds)	Cost to Bring on a New Agent (dollars)
Presales Information	$10.23	18%	53%	5.58	36	$6,753
Order Taking and Tracking	$7.90	31%	60%	7.51	40	$4,335
Technical Support	$15.92	22%	50%	7.14	66	$7,316

©BenchmarkPortal, Inc.

Figure 16. This figure categorizes call center performance metrics by the most typical functions provided by telephone agents. Notice that turnover is the lowest in the least stressful function, namely, pre-sales information, and the highest in order taking and tracking situations.

Promotions within the Organization

While anyone that has worked in customer service knows that customer service experience is an ideal way to become intimately familiar with the company, this approach creates unique challenges for the contact center manager. In companies where this issue isn't directly addressed, the turnover effect can have as much of an impact as if CSRs were walking out the door.

We have found that a better approach to promotions, especially if a company routinely recruits from the customer service contact center, is to plan for the movement through anticipatory hiring. Calculate how much of the overall turnover rate is tied to in-company promotions, and include the equivalent number of CSRs in the anticipatory hiring rate. From our experience, here is an important point. Make sure you include the learning-curve time, which is the time it takes for CSR to be at least 75% productive. Also, you should try to get some budgetary relief for the recruiting and training cost that you incur in finding and cultivating these great people that others are recruiting from your center.

We have also found that in the companies where this approach works well, there is usually a specified time period before the new employee can move on to a new department and a new job. The contact center has invested time and energy training the new hire and needs to recoup the investment with some period of productive time. The time factor varies based on how complex the business is, and the length of the learning curve before a new hire is productive.

CSR Career Planners - Advancement Idea that Goes to the Next Level.

Some companies provide Career Planners for CSRs. The Career Planner works with anyone on the team in a variety of career development planning activities. In some cases, they provide aptitude testing to help CSRs learn more about themselves and possible future career options. In other cases, they help find resources for additional education. Within the organization, the Career Planner is well versed on all the departments and the skill sets needed. They may set up "shadowing" sessions (CSR observes another role for a half/full day) or informational interviews to better understand the new job. Overall, the role exists to reinforce the organizations commitment to helping CSRs develop and grow in whatever direction is best for them. It reinforces the care for the person, ahead of the care of the position or the company.

Case study

At Autodesk Inc., the software developer in San Rafael, CA, trainers are rolling out a retention workshop on the company Intranet. The goal is to mold the company's 300 U.S. managers into career counselors. The workshop, still in development, will instruct managers to meet regularly with staffers, to clarify workers' wants and values, and to discuss promotion or opportunities in other departments. Managers will then create a development plan for each employee, complete with specific steps on a fixed timeline.[16]

Career advancement--doesn't always mean a direct promotion.

Discuss with each employee what he or she is looking for personally. Some other career enriching and advancement ideas are as follows:

- Lateral (moving across) involves a change in job, but not necessarily a change in responsibility.

- Exploratory (investigating possibilities) requires answering questions like "What else can I do?"

- Enrichment (growing in place) recommends that the current job can be fertile ground for growth and learning.

- Realignment (moving down) reconciles the demands of work with other priorities. Realignment can also imply getting back to the line job you loved before you got into management.

- Vertical (moving up) describes the traditional way to move-up. However, "up" is in short supply in most organizations.[23]

Educational Graffiti©

"Outstanding leaders go out of their way to boost the self-esteem of their personnel. If people believe in themselves, it's amazing what they can accomplish." Sam Walton

"Workers always give to the organization or firm in direct proportion to what they perceive themselves receiving from it." Jack Hawley

73

Verbatim comments from in-service practitioners in the Purdue Study:

"In our customer service department, we created the Career Institute, with very clear paths of promotional and lateral opportunities for our customer service representatives. We met with each CSR individually to identify which path best met their interests and abilities. Our skills development program has enabled us to fill most positions internally, which has had the greatest effect on retaining our best associates. The Career Institute has had a positive ripple effect throughout our contact center, as associates see their colleagues reaching their professional goals, and many are setting similar goals. Retention has increased dramatically since this program launched one year ago."

"We created a career ladder for our non-technical and technical/healthcare professional agents. This led to increased morale and job satisfaction and gave the agents something to strive for. The "promotion" to a higher level is based on a number of factors, most notably performance. When agents realize that they have an opportunity to progress within our organization, they are more willing to "dedicate" themselves. We also make the promotion event well known through the whole company."

"The most unique and compelling agent turnover reduction initiative was to set up multiple levels within the contact center for career advancement. Moving agents from junior to senior to specialist classes in their title adds value and pride to their position. Each level carries with it a slight pay increase that is more than offset by our improvements in agent retention."

Providing Effective Communication

We found that the manager's ability to communicate new information and vision to the CSRs is critical to create the trust and feeling of being "in on things." Here are some suggestions to improve your communications:

1. Make sure CSRs have the information they need, namely, updated resources, changes in products, anything related to effectively performing their job.

2. Make sure a customer never calls with news that the CSR should have already received, but did not. It's no fun to be in the "dark."

3. Share openly how the department, as well as the whole company, is performing.

4. Share the issues/concerns of the organization as a whole.

5. Make sure there are effective listening posts for CSRs to share what is really going on.

6. Make sure that quick action is taken on all good suggestions.

7. Make sure feedback is being given on a scheduled (not just "regular") basis.

8. Make sure each CSR has scheduled one-on-one time with their direct manager.

9. Make sure there are confidential avenues for grievances.

10. Make sure everyone knows about new job opportunities in the department and within the company.

In the contact center environment, change is one of the only constants. Whether it is changes to products, or adding new customers, or realignment of processes, CSRs are subject to constant change in their professional lives. Having the ability to communicate effectively through change is a critical component to keeping CSRs engaged and committed. The following sections

---

Educational Graffiti©

"No one enjoys addressing other people's deficiencies. But failure to do so sends the message that people are on track when they really aren't. And that may be the greatest disservice a leader can do to someone else." Eric Harvey

contain some of our tips to help you make sure your CSRs are getting what they need from you.

Change Management Communication

When significant change is happening, or is going to happen, communication is even more important. Make sure your communication is effective in giving people what they want to know and what they really need to know about how the change will affect their working lives.

This is an area where the direct relationship with the first line leader is critical. If there is an established level of trust, the team will feel less anxiety when their manager reassures them. A large portion of the anxiety during change is created by the "we don't know what we don't know" factor--meaning that, in the absence of information, people will come to their own (usually incorrect) conclusions.

There is an acronym which helps to illustrate the frame of mind during change. FEAR represents "Fantasized Events Appearing Real." An effective retention champion helps his/her team understand what is real and what is imagined. The next section outlines some basic guidelines to help manage the communication process during times of change.

What CSRs Want

Empathy: Someone to listen to and legitimize their concerns, fears and issues. They don't need sympathy and agreement, merely listening and clarification.

Information. As much information as possible regarding the change. Also being told, "that's all I have right now...when I get more, I'll tell you."

Ideas. Plans, strategies, action items. Any method to deal with the change.

What CSRs Usually Get

Autocratic Behavior. Managers who just tell CSRs without getting them involved. Managers who implement plans and suggest ideas, and then just expect people to carry them out.

Avoidance. They often get the total absence of any empathy. When the organization displays no interest in people's feelings, the message is, "we don't care."

"Rah-Rah" Behavior. The tendency to stress the future positive outcomes of what is, at present, a negative experience.

Verbatim comments from in-service practitioners in the Purdue Study:

"Building trust with the staff at all levels. It's not something that happens overnight, but by having regularly scheduled communication briefings (45 to 60 minutes) of small-ish groups (15 to 20 max) of all levels of staff, you can give them lots of information, as well as address the "rumor mill" and other questions."

"This, as well as having a weekly communication vehicle - like a newsletter that contains column(s) by top management -reduces an "us vs. them" situation, by letting even the most junior staff feel they are privy to most, or all, of the same information as everyone else. No one can play "lord" over another person just because they know something that the other person does not. Communication is very vital to instilling trust and comfort amongst the staff."

The Right Incentives for the Desired Results

There are two areas to consider when designing performance-based pay incentives. First, you should provide incentives based on measurable and quantifiable performance and, second, you need to determine how annual merit dollars are distributed.

For performance-based dollars, consider that CSRs in a contact center environment are generally paid modest salaries. The best CSRs will excel in their performance when they believe that the company not only recognizes them personally for their contribution, but also demonstrates the additional value they bring to the organization.

The strategy of providing additional performance-based incentive dollars comes with the belief that the dollars invested in retaining the talent is money well spent. The alternative is to spend the dollars on turnover costs, namely recruiting, screening and training new-hires. Information from the Purdue Benchmark Research tells us that the cost of a new hire can be between $6,000 and $10,000, depending on the industry and the type of call handled.

When creating a performance-based incentive, start by determining the performance ranges to expect from everyone on the team. Then develop an "above threshold" metric for the behaviors to reward. For example, provide extra incentive dollars when the majority of a CSR's personal customers are extremely satisfied with the service received. Make sure everyone on the team understands the details of the program (specifically it must be crystal clear regarding the what, how, when and by whom). The program must be perceived as credible and attainable.

Be careful not to encourage efficiency-based metrics, such as average talk time, because "improvements" in this metric usually have a direct negative effect on overall caller satisfaction (i.e., CSRs will hurry callers off the phone).

The other area to consider is the performance appraisal. This annual review process should support the other retention activities by reinforcing the value each CSR brings to the organization. There are two areas where companies err and damage an otherwise effective system.

First, recognize that excellent CSRs will not be motivated to stay if the only incentive is an annual merit increase, especially if the difference between mediocre and exceptional is a marginal 1% to 4% difference (typical for most contact centers according to the Purdue Research). If the merit increase is really intended to be a "cost-of-living" increase, communicate honestly about the intent of the increase. Consider separating the performance appraisal from the annual salary "bump," especially if there is no perceived differential percent from one performance level to another.

Second, some companies try to apply a bell curve approach to all employees. This means there is a belief that the majority of employees should be rated as "expected" or "average." There are usually percentage targets of the number of employees within each division that are "allowed" to be "above average" or "exceptional." After all, the thinking goes, if they are all "above expected," isn't something wrong with our base expectations? We find this reasoning to be very narrow-minded and definitely "not with the program" of minimizing turnover.

In our opinion and experience, what these companies are missing is that no one ever strives to be a "C" (or average) student. Human nature dictates that we all want to be considered special and better than average. In a contact center environment, where the role each CSR plays is very critical to the satisfaction level of your customers, you want a team of individuals that is above average. There is also the human factor, which is that people aspire to the level you expect of them. A retention champion knows that, if each CSR honestly believes that the manager has faith in them to be an exceptional CSR, most CSRs will perform at their absolute best to live up to this expectation.

We often heard managers tell us "our people are our greatest asset." In fact, we know that many contact center leaders have said those words, but it is the companies that truly believe in these words that continually invest in their CSRs. As a CSR learns and grows, their value within the organization also increases.

Educational Graffiti©

"Our survey findings revealed 58% of exited employees felt they had poor communications with management." Anonymous

79

Literature Search Findings on Investing in CSRs

World-class companies embrace a philosophy of continuous training. Training hours are allotted for every front-line CSR (ranging from 90 to 150 hours annually) and are factored into the call demand forecasting and resource scheduling at least one year in advance.[14]

Front-line CSRs are empowered to resolve virtually all contacts. Front-line workers "own the contact" and first-contact resolution rates are 85% or greater, with customer requested hand-offs accounting for nearly all of the remainder. Front-line workers are expected to take whatever time is necessary to resolve a caller's issues. Individual contact handling time is not used for assessment of performance. Monetary write-off authority is high for front-line workers. At one large company it was equal to that of the vice presidents.[14]

Dick Leider says, "The biggest problem today isn't burnout, instead, it is "rust out." So many people in our organizations are capable of doing so much more than we've ever asked (or allowed) them to do. So let'em do it! The more ownership they assume for the responsibilities built into their job, the more likely they are to stay with it, no matter (and perhaps because of) how challenging they find it".[25]

When we cut our database and compare improvements brought on by investing in computer-assisted learning programs we come up with some interesting results regarding turnover. In figure 15 on page 63 you can see that having access to continuous learning modules can cut turnover by almost 50%.

Literature Search Findings on Best Practices in Telephone Service

Provide outcome-based pay incentives. A portion of pay for the front-line, support staff and management team is tied to meeting specific contact center performance targets for quality and quantity. Individual worker and management incentives are payable only when the entire center achieves the performance targets. Progress toward meeting the goals should be measured daily, and reviewed weekly and monthly. Incentives should be paid quarterly.[14]

The well being and personal satisfaction of a front-line CSR must be as high a priority within the organization as is caller satisfaction. The front-line CSR's working environment in successful contact centers is tied almost directly to achieving world-class service. Ergonomically designed furniture, adequate workspace, state-of-the-art workstations, the right tools, and an atmosphere for teaming and personal excellence are all common to world-class contact centers.[14]

Educational Graffiti©

"You can't hire people who don't apply." Anonymous

CHAPTER 5: HIRE SLOWLY...FIRE QUICKLY

What Does "Hire Slowly...Fire Quickly" Mean?

Simply put, this means spend time up-front to make sure offers made are to the absolute best candidates that exist. It also means, when someone is not working out, help him or her move on with his or her career (with another company) as soon as possible.

How to Hire Slowly...

Recognize that if a CSR has gone through an extensive selection process and is hired, there is more pride in being selected. It's similar to going through try-outs for a varsity sports team. Knowing that "only the best" are hired is also a factor in retaining the best talent. The Marine Corps once prided itself on its advertisement that "we need only a few good men." Today, the Marines include both men and women, but they still promote their "only the best" campaign with their advertisements, "be a part of the few, the proud, the Marines."

Hiring slowly doesn't mean that the process to bring people into the company has to be laborious and lengthy. It does mean that there is a thorough process in place to scrutinize the candidates and to assess them from many angles. It may mean screening out many candidates, but the process itself can be time-efficient.

The following nine steps increase the odds of hiring successful CSRs:

1. Define the ideal CSR for the environment.

- Consider the caliber of CSRs you need. Will an inexperienced, but energetic high school graduate be sufficient? Do you need someone who has had several prior positions serving customers, someone who understands how to separate issues from personalities?

- What is the brand image of the company? Do CSRs need to project a neighborhood friendly image, or a state-of-the-art technically advanced image?

- Identify the best CSRs in your contact center. Determine the distinguishing aspects that apply to them (and not marginal CSRs). Incorporate questions and responses in the interview process that will determine if the applicant matches those aspects.

- What skill level is needed? Is the position primarily order entry or is extensive problem solving required?

- Or, does it require extensive system navigation? How much multi-tasking is required?

In addition to closely defining the skills, you need to define what personal traits would be ideal. We believe there are three main traits in an "ideal" CSR.

- **They must be intelligent**. A CSR role requires active thinking at all times. CSRs need to be able to think on their feet, act as a detective to read both direct and implied issues and to assimilate new information on a daily basis. To be highly effective, a higher than average intelligence level is required.

- **They must have a positive, "can do," attitude**. We've all heard the "hire for attitude, train for skill" philosophy. Attitude is something that is deeply engrained in a person's personality. If a person has a positive perspective, he/she carries the "whatever-it-takes approach" to every other aspect of their job.

- **They must have a "need to serve."** Most of the best CSRs are drawn to positions of helping others. Look for patterns in their work and hobby history. Some may have been day care providers or Sunday school teachers. Find people with "service-in-their-heart"...people who truly enjoy helping others.

2. Get creative in the recruitment process.

Make sure the best candidates are being considered. One company described the process of only interviewing people who approached the companies as being the same as a professional team relying only on players that showed up to try out for a sport. Don't rely on "walk-ons." By total exception, one of these "might" work out, but don't count on it.

The overall best approach is referral by current (highly valued) employees. There are several reasons this is so effective. The current employee:

- will not refer someone that they would not want as a co-worker.

- would not refer someone that would be a negative reflection on them.

If the referred person is hired, there can be built-in peer pressure to excel. You may benefit from some friendly competition between the two.

Another important benefit is that the people referred are usually already employed and are not watching the want ads. You might not otherwise have the opportunity to consider them.

We found that many companies have a referral bonus program. For example, if the company hires someone referred by an employee, that employee receives a monetary bonus. If the referred new hire is still employed after six months, the referring employee will receive another monetary bonus. Great concept.

"If You Find Them, They Will Come."

Another way (one of our favorites) is to always be on the lookout for exceptional service providers. Keep in mind your definition of the ideal CSR. When you experience

Educational Graffiti©

"Everyone has an invisible sign hanging around their neck saying, 'Make me feel important.'" Mary Kay Ash

exceptional service, thank the person and invite them to apply at your company. Create a simple business card that states:

> Thank you for our excellent service.
>
> We are always looking for exceptional people to join our team.
>
> If you're interested, please contact _____ at _____ and let them know you were given this card by _____.

Keep the card generic and give a supply to your team. You may want to consider giving the option to refer others to those who have proven themselves (especially if there is a referral bonus involved).

Again, the best candidates may be people that are not actively looking for a new position. They may be ideal employees because they are good at what they do and are happy doing it. Unless someone comes along to present an opportunity, they would happily provide exceptional service for their current company.

While we have found that placing help wanted ads is important and is the standard/traditional way to announce openings, we have also found that ads produce hit-and-miss results. When writing the ad, consider emphasizing the ideal traits for your company. For example, "We're looking for someone who is high energy, can multi-task, is able to develop creative solutions quickly and gets along well with almost everyone." By your being this honest, some candidates will self-screen themselves out.

3. Start with a computerized interview.

Today, most contact centers test keyboarding skills and speed using computerized testing. To get a fuller view of the candidates, consider screening for overall qualifications. For example, Marriott Hotels use self-administered tests. The computer asks:

- Why did you leave your last job?
- How would you rate your performance?
- How often do you get frustrated at work?
- How well do you get along with superiors?
- How would you rate your organizational skills?
- Do other people say you're flexible?

To each question, the candidate types in a multiple choice answer. After the applicant leaves, the computer spews out not a verdict but a list of questions to be asked during a subsequent interview, questions like "Why did the candidate rate his/her organizational skills as only "average"? The printout also notes any time an applicant paused longer than usual to ponder a question, on the theory that hesitation usually indicates that the candidate may be hiding something. The software poses the sort of personality-probing questions that managers often have trouble asking. It also seems to encourage candor.[15]

4. Conduct a telephone interview.

We were amazed that many contact centers skip this step. If a candidate doesn't have a pleasing voice, or isn't able to communicate clearly on the telephone, they don't have the necessary "job-related" traits and skills to be hired. When conducting the telephone interview, listen for the following elements:[22]

Volume	Speech pace	Clear pronunciation
Grammar mistakes	Interesting tone	Nasal/Whine
Monotone	Listening ability	Quick comprehension
Takes control	Accent	Clear thoughts
Enthusiasm	Empathy	Sense of caring

Educational Graffiti©

"People want to feel what they do makes a difference." Francis Hesselbein

87

5. Have a trained interviewer conduct a personal interview.

Determine who owns the in-person interview process. It may be a team of managers that rotate. Make sure each one is trained in successful interviewing approaches.

We found that many companies simply rely on the managers to conduct the interviews without equipping them with any "tools" to use when interviewing. There are specific interviewing techniques that go well beyond asking "behavioral" or "situational" questions to determine whether or not a candidate will be successful. There is a skill to asking uncommon questions and knowing what to look for in the responses. Also, knowing when to probe deeper and where the legal limits lie are important. Even having skills in reading body language can add an extra aspect of assessment.

6. Complete a personality profile.

If there are specific personality profiles that help define the ideal CSR, consider having applicants complete a personality profile test. Many of the personality testing companies have done extensive studies on the profiles of successful CSRs. Some even have profiles specifically for contact center roles. There may also be matches to your defined ideal CSR within the basic Myers Briggs personality typing (for example, many CSRs are strong in the "feeling" category).

7. Conduct a reality check review.

Before an offer is made, make sure the candidate is given honest information about the position and understands the expectations of the job. Here are examples of information to share:

- the organization's mission and vision-especially of contact center
- compensation and benefits-both now and future
- description of a typical day
- aspects of the job that other CSRs find difficult
- aspects of the job that other CSRs find rewarding
- opportunities of development/training

- expectations around time-off (especially holidays)
- expectations around overtime requirements
- expectations about shift changes.

Consider even having the candidate spend some time in the actual work environment sitting with a positive CSR. We refer to this as a "realistic job preview." Since the hiring process is a two-way process and the candidate is also deciding whether or not s/he wants to accept the role, it is important that the candidate be exposed to as many facets of the role as possible before accepting. This is especially important if the candidate has no prior contact center experience.

8. Conduct background and reference checks.

Even though a candidate may pass all selection criteria, be sure to check their background. Ask for more than business references. Ask for personal and association references as well. Although, some references may only answer with "confirm or deny" responses, some will give personal perspectives on a candidate's strengths as well as weaknesses.

9. Make an offer with clear expectations.

Consider documenting the "hiring expectations." Many times, especially in contact centers, there is miscommunication about what was promised when someone was hired. Some of the confusion happens around the time when the first raise in pay should happen. Also, we found a lot of confusion about what is required to be promoted to the next level, and what requirements there are before being allowed to apply for positions outside the department.

Educational Graffiti©

"There is something that is much more scarce, something rarer than ability. It is the ability to recognize ability." Robert Half

---

<u>Hiring CSRs - Basic Traits to Look for:</u>[3]

Expectations of CSRs (by Customers)
- Be polite and courteous.
- Be friendly and professional.
- Listen and respond to customers' needs.
- Be interested and willing to help.
- Avoid jargon. Use language the customer understands.
- Be accessible, provide prompt service.
- Be honest. Present self as believable and trustworthy.
- Set realistic expectation and deliver what they promise.
- Have the knowledge and skills needed to complete the transaction.

To meet these expectations, hire people who:
- Possess a service attitude
- Learn quickly and have a commitment to life-long learning
- Can adapt to a rapidly changing environment
- Have outstanding verbal and written communication skills
- Pay attention to detail and quality
- Can conduct business and be cordial
- Appear genuine and interested during phone conversations
- Listen and capture essential customer information
- Have keyboarding skills
- Enjoy working with people.

We have found that, with all the above "good stuff," you can easily train CSRs in your products and service specifics.

How to Fire Quickly...

Most people don't enjoy conflict. But, being responsible for the overall performance of a contact center requires dealing with situations that can be uncomfortable. In the long run, it's best to address issues as they come up, as quickly and directly as possible. Having a non-performer on the team brings down the morale of the entire team. If the team observes that no action is taken, the work culture becomes diluted because being a high performing team is no longer the standard. This also erodes the team's respect for your leadership.

To fire quickly, the contact center needs:

- clear expectations and feedback process
- established discipline guidelines
- credible review process to ensure due diligence
- authority within the contact center to take action on terminations
- established (and communicated) guidelines for zero tolerance* situations, like:

  > *swearing at a customer
  > *hanging up on a customer
  > *disconnecting contacts
  > *unprofessional behavior with co-workers.

Here is an example dialogue from a Gallup study:

Gallup: "Have you ever fired anyone?"

Michael: "Unfortunately, I have. Like most managers, sometimes I don't pick the right people and things start to fall apart."

Gallup: "What is your approach to firing an employee?"

Michael: "Do it fast, the faster the better. If someone is consistently under-performing, you might think you are doing him or her a favor by waiting. You aren't. You're actually making matters worse."[7]

Educational Graffiti©

"The essence of leadership is the capacity to build and develop the self-esteem of the workers." Irwin Federman

Case study of The Container Store[16]

Many of the company's employees come from its large supply of satisfied customers. Employees are encouraged to hand out gold cards to friendly customers. These business-card-sized invitations have a phone number and say simply, "The most organized store in America is looking for a few neat people."

The company provides 235 hours of training for its first-year, full-time employees. "This level of training also allows customers to feel as if they're dealing with a manager, regardless of the person's position."

They pay 50 to 100% more than the industry average (except to top executives). Their philosophy:

- One average employee does the work of three lousy employees.
- One good employee does the work of three average employees.
- One great employee does the work of three good employees.

Case study in hiring

Horst Schultz, CEO of the Ritz Carlton, said in a speech that when an employee did not succeed in the company and had to be terminated, it was the company's fault for not doing its job in the hiring process. Part of the Ritz-Carlton mission statement says, "We are ladies and gentlemen serving ladies and gentlemen." According to Mr. Schultz, only ladies and gentlemen are hired; therefore, they are treated as such from the first day of their employment."[16]

Comments from in-service practitioners in the Purdue Study:

"We have put significantly more effort into defining the correct employee profile and recruiting and screening intensely for these characteristics."

"We changed our hiring profile from high-speed, technical go-getters who expected an administration/engineering position after three to six months to customer service-orientated, long-term career path type persons who expect to be on the help desk for at least one to two years. This reduced our turnover tremendously and improved our customer relations."

"We are being extremely selective when interviewing candidates to take a contact center position. Most people have an open position and scramble to fill it as soon as possible. They interview five people and take the best one. We tell our HR department what we are looking for, they screen for us, and then we interview between 15 to 20 candidates."

"We instituted a highly selective recruiting procedure."

"We emphasize effective screening of candidates. Potential employees need to know what they will be faced with in the contact center environment and should be told up front what the challenges will be. In addition, skill assessments must be conducted to determine if the candidate has the base skills needed to be successful in the contact center."

"Our contact center is in India. Giving the agents the ability to rotate shifts was the most significant aspect that led to increased satisfaction and ultimately to decreased turnover."

Educational Graffiti©
"If you don't give people information, they'll make up something to fill the void."
Carla O'Dell

Comments from in-service practitioners in the Purdue Study: (continued)

"We try to really promote the family atmosphere and flexible scheduling (for schooling and family activities). We are a small contact center, so we do a rotating shift where they work 7:30 to 5 Monday through Thursday, and 8 to 2 on Friday (no lunch). They really enjoy being off for half of the day. As we anticipate growing, we are hoping to go to four 10-hour days or do something creative with 9-hour shifts."

"I have found that flex scheduling has helped our staff tremendously. It's not easy to schedule, but it does allow the agents to alter their schedules as needed."

"To combat 50% annual turnover in a tight Atlanta job market, we took the step of reducing the workweek of contact center employees from 40 to 30 hours - with the same pay! We now have less than 5% annual negative attrition and no problems attracting new job applicants."

Literature Search Findings on Hiring and Firing

In world-class companies (for example, USAA), intense screening of CSRs makes it impossible for new-hires to "touch" the customer unless they have passed all the proficiency tests.

A casting director for Disney said, "We're looking for personality. We can train for skills. We want people who are enthusiastic, who have pride in their work, who can take charge of a situation without supervision."[15]

Literature Search Findings on Best Practices in Telephone Service

We found that highly-selective hiring practices identify applicants who fit the culture and value system of the organization. Companies that are in-the-know, hire new workers and fully train them prior to anticipated need dates. In this environment there are typically no human resource shortfalls to contend with – planning is everything. An extensive array of recognition programs helps to encourage high levels of participation in individual and team performance improvement activities. Training is based on detailed new-hire needs analyses which are linked to achieving the organization's stated mission and vision, as well as strategic goals and objectives.[14]

Educational Graffiti©

"Communicate everything to your associates. The more they know, the more they care. Once they care, there is no stopping them." Sam Walton

95

CHAPTER 6: ROOT CAUSES OF AGENT TURNOVER

Turnover Root Cause Assessment Methodology

In applying our methodology at real customer contact centers, we discovered the following:

1. The root cause of CSR turnover was always a uniquely different combination of management, policy, technology, location, hiring/screening, and other factors.

2. Getting the real root cause to surface took painstaking time and on-site research.

3. The on-site root cause research was best done by a trusted "outsider" capable of building individual confidence with the CSRs.

4. The return on invested time and money (ROI) was always over 100% in the first year.

We have summarized our three-phased methodology below:

Phase I -- Initial On-Site Visit and Kick-Off Meetings

1. Capture and analyze "existing" Human Resources data, namely:

   - Determine figures for voluntary versus involuntary turnover.

   - Determine figures for internal versus external turnover.

   - Determine if there are areas with higher turnover than normal.

   - Determine if turnover is seasonal.

   - Determine if there is a trend of turnover as related to time on the job, i.e., length of employment.

   - Study exit interview reports.

2. Collect "one-step removed" feedback data, namely:

- Talk with professionals in Human Resources who actually conducted exit interviews and document any "off the record" insights they may have.

- Talk with former phone agents who left the contact center for other jobs within your contact center, i.e., those who are still vested, but who are far enough away from contact center management to be candid about their experience. Separate this group into those phone agents that took a promotion as they left the contact center, vis-à-vis those that took a lateral move to another job within your company.

- Talk with trainers, senior CSRs, Team Leads, and others who might act as confidants to CSRs.

3. Review processes within contact center Human Resources, namely:

- recruiting, screening, and interviewing
- new employee orientation
- new employee training
- on-going development of existing employees
- expectation setting
- feedback methods
- communication channels
- benefits
- promotion criteria
- career mapping alternatives.

4. Collect and research profile information on past phone agents, namely:

- those valued employees who left voluntarily during the last six to nine months

- those marginal phone agents who left voluntarily during the last six to nine months

- determine if there are trends, profiles, similarities and clues to turnover.

5. Contact a statistical sample of former phone agents who left voluntarily and gather their feedback by mail, e-mail or, preferably, telephone.

6. Collect feedback from front-line CSRs, namely:

    • Use a specific contact-designed survey process to get highest percent response and most candid results.

    • Ask for suggestions of the "informal leaders" that will share more cogent information and who act as representatives for the CSR team.

7. Collect feedback from the front-line leadership team, namely, supervisors and team leaders. Also review success criteria for leadership, namely, the bonus structure and other benefits/perks related to retention.

8. Establish a "safety zone" for additional feedback from the CSRs as they may informally discuss our survey and information-gathering process and have additional insights.

9. Conduct more in-depth interviews with select groups, namely, informal leaders identified by CSRs.

10. Sit side-by-side with additional front-line CSRs. Build trust and a forum for casual sharing.

Phase Two -- Off-Site Behind the Scenes Analysis

1. Compile and analyze all captured and discovered information.

2. Compare findings to benchmark data and known best practices of Human Resources.

3. List all potential root causes of turnover at your contact center.

4. Determine most critical root causes, namely, those in the "must fix now" category.

Educational Graffiti©

"Tell me and I'll forget; show me and I may remember; involve me and I'll understand." Chinese Proverb

"There are two things that people want more than sex and money - recognition and praise." Mary Kay Ash

Phase Three -- Validate Root Causes and Determine Potential and Realistic Solutions

1. Investigate and ensure the validity of each of the final root causes.

2. Determine what behaviors cause CSR perceptions.

3. Collect additional data as indicated by initial findings. For example, if, CSRs feel like there aren't enough advancement opportunities, review the up-front expectation setting (what are they told when they're hired)? What opportunities are there? Could others be developed? Is the staffing level adequate to allow for growth training?

4. Quantify all critical root cause findings.

We gathered these comments and suggestions in a survey of thousands of contact center professionals. We asked the question:

"What is one idea that you have seen work in reducing agent turnover and improving long-term employee retention?"

The responses are organized into "The Top Ten" categories. We repeated some responses in more than one category when the response addressed more than one area.

There was one message that really captured the reason we decided to delve into this topic. It describes a culture that is more prevalent than any of us would like to believe. We appreciate this respondent's candor:

"My company has been groping for a viable methodology to reduce turnover ever since its creation; however, (alas) to date we still experience a **500%** turnover rate and all the costs associated with this reality. Fundamentally, **our problem stems from our managerial inability to recognize that one must give in order to receive.** Indeed, our attitudes and treatment of our representatives would **constitute the perfect MBA program case study of what not to do** (comprehensively) in managing human resources. This problem is common for outbound teleservices companies because the sales mentality dictates success is based on doing what one can get away with rather than doing what is right."

1. Turning Managers (into Retention Champions)

"Remember that while we may have hired employees, we got people instead. We can't forget the human element."

"It's not all about pay. It's about creating an environment where the employee feels valued and part of a community."

"Employee recognition and expressed sincere appreciation from the management level will help to greatly reduce turnover. Another excellent method is to get to know the employee and understand what motivates them. Some want words of affirmation while others want gifts or one-on-one time with the manager. This can produce significant results."

"Understanding that the biggest key to keeping good people is providing them one-on-one interaction with their boss. We use the phrase, 'it's the boss, stupid,' time and again to make sure our team leaders know that people won't stay because of center level incentives if they hate their boss. People might seek out a job because of pay, benefits, etc., but if their boss makes them miserable every day, they won't stick around."

"We promote an inclusive management leadership style and a team approach to our operations."

"When I was just starting out in the contact center industry, I worked in one of four contact centers for a major credit union. My contact center was the worst. The people didn't care. They just showed up to do the job. We got a new manager a month after I joined. He really listened and was supportive. He asked us what *we* thought when we brought him customer situations. He asked good questions when needed. After a while, a rep knew if s/he were good because he'd listen, then just approve the recommendation. He empowered us, and he made work fun. The other back office departments didn't understand the challenges we customer service reps faced, and frequently would not readily help us or they would direct us somewhere else. My manager implemented a new theme: 'Actually, it is my job!' Not only did we feel empowered to resolve situations that we might have been passed on, but we had also fun with the slogan: 'It's Friday, it's not my job today,' and 'Is that YOUR job? Why yes, actually it is!' Within six months, we were the best contact center. We were damn good, took pride in our work, resolved issues better, led in loan dollars. Sure, there was turnover. A lot of it was due to internal promotions. But within the contact centers, people were reluctant to leave that particular contact center. So, I think that to pick one thing that contributed to the success of that contact center and that reduced turnover, it was *empowerment!*"

"We have replaced monetary incentives with employee-focused activities. We have made a concerted effort to develop the whole employee rather than just the person we see at work."

"Building trust with the staff- at all levels is not something that happens over night. This, as well as having a weekly communication vehicle like a newsletter that contains column(s) by top management reduces an "us vs. them" situation, by letting even the most junior staff feel they are privy to most or all of the same information that everyone else is. No one can play "lord" over another person just because they know something that the other person does not. Communication is very vital to instilling trust and comfort amongst the staff."

"When dealing with agents, we are more successful when management takes an active role, as opposed to a hands off approach."

"Management replacement significantly changed agent attitudes and work behaviors."

"Two of the elements key to our success are (1) an accent on "We implemented this to build a work environment that allows employees to accomplish their goals and be fulfilled in their work. This is achieved through a process of feedback that promotes a dialog between managers and staff so that action is taken to ensure that employees:

- know what is expected of them at work
- have the tools and materials they need to do their jobs right
- receive recognition for doing good work
- have their voices heard, and are involved in decision making
- can learn, grow, and fulfill their career goals within the company."

"We had regular meetings with the General Manager."

"There's no initiative or magic bullet. Make the call center a place where people want to work!"

"Prior to my being manager here, agents were constantly searching for other jobs. Since I have been Contact Center Manager, I have not had any agents leave for other jobs. However, we did have a large layoff this past year and a retirement incentive program, which reduced my staff significantly. Of the employees that remain, the reason for doing so seems to be having an open door policy where employees can discuss concerns with management and experience group participation."

"Approximately two years ago, our CEO allowed the implementation of an initiative within our contact center that we believe is unique. To combat 50% annual turnover in a tight Atlanta job market, we took the step of reducing the workweek of contact center employees from 40 to 30 hours with the same pay! We now have less than 5% annual negative attrition and no problems attracting new job applicants. In addition, the experience level, job satisfaction and reduction in job stress for our reps have all been impacted positively. The savings of no longer having to constantly replace reps has offset the budgetary costs of increasing our staff to make up for the hours of converting to a 30-hour workweek."

"We use a mix of full-time and part-time agents to counteract turnover and deal with a fluctuating workload. We offer flexible hours for the part-time agents to accommodate their schedules. Our flexibility and the fact that they are not working 40 hours per week helps us avoid agent burnout and turnover."

2. Individualizing the CSR Experience

"Treat the phone representatives as if they are the most important part of your organization, because they are!"

"Recognize that customer service representatives are an integral part of the organization."

"Take the time to say, 'thank you'."

"Once a month we CSRs had "skip" meetings (supervisors were skipped) to share information. We also created an Advisory Committee to help our management solve the tough issues."

"Vice Presidents, Directors, Managers, and Supervisors need to show sincere appreciation for the job Technical Support Specialists perform."

"Turnover drops when staff feels appreciated and respected. The help desk often gets little respect or rewards."

"There is a need for better feedback and appreciation by supervisors and managers."

"If representatives are happy in their positions and acknowledged for their accomplishments, they rarely look for other opportunities, much less leave for other positions. Our initiative is ongoing to address morale issues and acknowledge/reward individual performance. Some of the components are an 'Employee of the Month award,' instant recognition for customer commendations, early-leave points awarded to representatives caught in the act of delighting our customers, and 15 minutes of our monthly meeting devoted to kudos."

"Recognition of employees' contributions and sincere appreciation from management helps greatly to reduce turnover. Another excellent action is to get to know the employee and understand what language they speak. Some want words of affirmation, while others want gifts or one-on-one time with the manager. Such a program reaps significant results. Something that worked for us was celebrating excellence in customer service with a week of activities culminating in a special event hosted by our CEO."

"Recognition for a job well done is extremely important."

"We try to really promote a family atmosphere and flexible scheduling (for schooling and family activities). We are a small contact center, so we do a rotating shift where agents work 7:30 to 5, Monday through Thursday and 8 to 2 on

Friday (no lunch). The agents really enjoy being off for half of the day. As we anticipate growing, we hope to go to four 10-hour days or do something creative with 9-hour shifts. We try to initiate activities that recognize the level of support the Customer Service Representative gives our customers."

"We provide career opportunities for advancement in job title and pay to top performers. We provide recognition to the entire contact center when department goals are met. And we reward top CSR's with incentives. Lastly, we create a fun work environment."

"We also have appropriate staffing so that if we are down one person, we can survive for a month. We treat our people with respect and try very hard to work with them when they need time off or have an emergency."

"We focus on empowerment of agents, employee participation in contact center changes and strategies, cross-training opportunities with our operations area and a revamped coaching system."

"Reducing turnover is a difficult task in a contact center environment. The problem with contact centers is that we have too many statistics, and it becomes very easy to treat an employee as a statistic. That, in turn, decreases morale and increases turnover. Creating processes to counteract this may help. Reward and recognition seems to be the remedy for just about anything. Treat employees as individuals instead of statistics. Use the statistics to manage your business, but reward individuals for good behaviors, not good statistics."

"Some form of appreciation really counts."

"We promote an inclusive management/leadership style and development of a team approach to contact center operations."

"Every two weeks all contact center employees fill out a survey. If scores are low, we can see the warning signs early and are able to try to give individuals extra attention. The feedback helps us change processes and procedures as a result of the feedback. It's worked great."

"We provide advanced training on customer service, relationship building and sales. We include CSRs in planning and implementing service/contact center initiatives."

"From our once-a-year Voice of Employee survey, we found that employees would like to have more flexibility on time off. Based on this input we altered our policies to allow employees more freedom and flexibility in determining their time off. We designed a program where employees are accountable for themselves and for business needs."

"People like to know that the harder they work, the more they will be rewarded. We have incorporated this philosophy into our work environment. The only departure I experienced this year was one agent who was selected for the Secret Service. This was a lifelong dream for him."

"The average age in our technical help desk contact center (250 seats) is 20 years old. We just make it a fun environment with parties and attractive incentives (movie vouchers, drinks, t-shirts). We are very flexible with working hours and desk environment. We listen to them and use their own idea's to improve their working environment as well as the way we handle customers."

"When I was just starting out in the contact center industry, I worked in one of four contact centers for a major credit union. My contact center was the worst. The people didn't care. They just showed up to do the job. We got a new manager a month after I joined. He really listened and was supportive. He asked us what *we* thought when we brought him customer situations. He asked good questions when needed. After a while, a rep knew if s/he were good because he'd listen, then just approve the recommendation. He empowered us, and he made work fun. The other back office departments didn't understand the challenges we customer service reps faced, and frequently would not readily help us or they would direct us somewhere else. My manager implemented a new theme: 'Actually, it is my job!' Not only did we feel empowered to resolve situations that we might have been passed on, but we had also fun with the slogan: 'It's Friday, it's not my job today,' and 'Is that YOUR job? Why yes, actually it is!' Within six months, we were the best contact center. We were damn good, took pride in our work, resolved issues better, led in loan dollars. Sure, there was turnover. A lot of it was due to internal promotions. But within the contact centers, people were reluctant to leave that particular contact center. So, I think that to pick one thing that contributed to the success of that contact center and that reduced turnover, it was *empowerment.*"

"We monitor contacts heavily. We found that the more positive feedback we'd give to our staff, the happier they are. It seems to have had a definite impact on our turnover. We also make the staff aware of where we are performance wise and solicit their input as to how we can improve. Making the CSR's feel a part of the team has also been a big help. If you show that you appreciate their hard work they seem to want to work harder and go the extra mile to serve our customers."

"Communication and participation are the best ways to reduce agent attrition. I implemented a program whereby the business plan for the coming 18 months is personally communicated to each of 50 agents in groups of 4. I seek their input and feedback. This allows them to better understand who the company is and where it is heading. The agents are more committed to their role and they see how and where they add value to the overall strategy. Also, we introduced the Managers Challenge whereby the agents are provided with a theme to decorate the center or come up with a catch phrase that mirrors the morale and psyche of the center. We also involve them in lead generation programs with a reward structure."

"We make our agents feel important and let them know that that they make a difference."

"Because we are supporting a fixed-price government contract, there are limitations to what we can do in the areas of compensation and training. We focused on internal appreciation programs for our agents. Specifically, we instituted an 'Agent of the Month' award. The winner's picture was published in the base newspaper. The winner also received little things like a free lunch with the boss.

"We also established a 'kudos' program (an on-the-spot award that any customer or staff member could make) and some cross training and mentoring and schedule rotation of the teams (i.e., desktop support would work with network support for a day, etc.)."

"We involve the agents in development and achievement of company goals. During the process of defining what the initiatives will be for the coming year, we hold brainstorming sessions (with sticky pads to ensure full involvement and anonymity) for ideas. We boil those down to three to five initiatives. Once the executive team outlines the annual initiatives for the company, we brainstorm again to identify how our team will be able to affect those initiatives and outline our specific goals for the quarter. This ensures ownership, accountability and immediate communication of the goals. This makes employees at all levels feel like they have a part in the direction and decision making of the company. "Based on their skills, agents may be involved in planning stages and interact face to face with the client. This provides the agent with a deeper understanding of the business he/she is going to interact with."

"Another thing we do is monitor total contacts for the day, maximum wait times, abandoned contacts, etc. We look at all the statistics. We try to catch our employees "doing something right." We always try to praise them for anything that goes well, to assure them that they know they are appreciated for the day-to-day excellent customer service they give. A major complaint in most contact centers is that they only hear when something is done wrong, but never about all the day-to-day right things they do."

"You need to make the job as much fun as possible, listen and invite feedback from associates to get their buy-in and a lot of positive feedback."

"Whenever there is a new initiative, project, website design, materials design, etc., we ask specifically for representative feedback. This has to be supported by upper management; however, we take the customer contacts so we affect the changes in our communication. The representatives feel like they have ownership in the process."

"Let the agents put improvements in process and let them work on implementation whenever possible. Then, the ideas come from the people on the phones, and they get the exposure to the continuous improvement needed on a help desk."

"We provide more discretionary, decision-making responsibility to staff integrated with a visible career-path."

"We rely on salary increases and empowerment of employees to assist in selecting their schedule and training."

"I developed and implemented an incentive and recognition program that resulted in lowering an 80% annual turnover rate to less than 7% annual turnover (due to terminations and resignations combined). My incentive ideas have since been written about in *The Customer Service Advantage*, a CS management newsletter. I also strongly believe in caring for and valuing your employees. Incentives and recognition don't mean anything to employees if they don't feel you are genuine in your appreciation."

"I elevated agents' salaries to a level that is higher than for similar positions in the organization. This helped keep turnover down and brought in more internal applications for new openings."

"My best results have come from a combination of techniques: communicating expectations, practicing flexibility on coaching methods, providing honest and positive feedback on a regular basis, not profiling the reps (treating each person with respect and not lumping them all into a single category), and consistent adherence to guidelines (rules). I had great success when I created a career path and opportunities for growth and career development for the help desk agents. More valuable pay-off came from providing and paying for additional training and classes. Involving the help desk in the development process and other projects that impact the help desk gave the employees the chance to participate and made them more interested and involved in their work."

"A few of the keys to successful relationships with agents are to have clear and simple goals, provisions for recognition, discipline, communication, birthday cards, friendly competition, strong leadership, quality feedback, potlucks, raises in a timely fashion, coaching, delegating, and showing career progression."

"We have empowered our agents with cross-training opportunities within our operations area and a revamped coaching system."

"We suggest giving the contact center professional an on-going task that is unrelated to answering calls. This gives him/her a break and an opportunity to be creative while working on another project. The project can be assigned by management or suggested by the employee, i.e., recommended telephone procedures, small programming tasks, designing forms, surveying the other staff to get improvement ideas, etc. Management has a responsibility to reaffirm to the contact center staff their worth to the organization. Management needs to remember these employees hear complaints all day long, which can be mentally draining."

"Our techniques include frequent feedback on agents' performance and contributions."

"We rely on increased compensation coupled with recognition of support role for Help Desk personnel."

"The purpose of the program is to build a work environment that allows employees to accomplish their goals and be fulfilled in their work. This is achieved through a process of feedback that promotes a dialog between managers and staff so that action is taken to ensure that employees: know what is expected of them at work; have the tools and materials they need to do their jobs right; receive recognition for doing good work; have their voices heard and are involved in decision making; and can learn, grow, and fulfill their career goals within the company."

"We provide professional and knowledge growth possibilities through training and modification of duties. We include the agents in the decisions regarding their particular direction (for training and for new duties)."

"We provide each agent with a daily P&L. In my opinion, this is compelling because it provides the agents with direct ownership of their impact on the company. Agents want to know that what they do makes a difference. This allows them to see it clearly."

"One of our contact centers was having a major problem with turnover because many of the customer service representatives were having a problem finding quality, affordable day care for their children. Working with various resources like the county, day care providers, etc., we were able to develop a network of information on day care services and providers. This had a significant impact on reducing turnover."

"For a noteworthy performance or action, an agent earns 15 minutes to use at their discretion within the next quarter. It can be accumulated or taken as earned. Each representative that earns time receives a large sign/plaque to be hung in their cubicle. This lets everyone know who is producing. Agents who exceed their performance goals receive give gift certificates on a monthly basis. It's important to reward and praise each representative individually. Treating agents as adults pushes them to strive higher and stick with the company. We are a major servicer in the mortgage industry. and our representatives are consistently on a contact campaign (inbound/outbound)."

"Our corporation offers many benefits to help them grow professionally while encouraging self-growth. Tuition assistance is one benefit that many take advantage of."

3. Provide Clear and Balanced Expectations

"We implemented a Customer Satisfaction incentive bonus plan allowing for increasing bonuses year after year based on customer satisfaction achievement levels. Based on customer satisfaction performance, an employee can earn 5K after one year, 10K after 2 years, 15K after 3 years and 20K after 4 years. Performance that is rewarded against corporate customer amounts have inherent retention incentive. Costs are justified by reduced cost of turnover, productivity gains of having more experienced agents, and long-term profitability of the corporation through improved customer satisfaction and loyalty. This plan has reduced turnover from 31% to 17%."

"We started with goals (not stretch) that appeared reasonable. The employees were advised that the goals are not final but only a start. In order to meet the company goals, we must do better but we needed to build some history and measure some results. The goals were subsequently increased several times with minimal objections by the collection staff, including those who had difficulty making their goals. Each time the bar was raised, so were the results. The success of raising the goals in a rather short period of time was a direct result of conducting regular and open communications/training meetings. These meetings are held twice a month (always on Friday, the lightest day for customer contacts). Refreshments are served and occasionally door prizes are given out. The meetings are scheduled for 30 minutes and are kept to that time limit with rare exception."

"In three separate instances I've seen agent turnover rates dropping by 7%, 10% and 8% after introduction of formal contact quality processes. This is more than a coincidence."

"We introduced the SITEL Management System (SMS) which enabled us to share agent performance data in a real-time basis, twice a day. We provide our people with clear, objective performance expectations. We report and track actual performance to those expectations and review them with the individual."

"When agents are trained and fully apprised of job requirements, positive and negative ramifications, they have a complete exposure of what they can expect to encounter in the day-to-day functions of the position. This approach will also negatively impact the number of trainees who accept the position, if it's a tough one, but the overall attrition rate is definitely minimized."

"We provide each agent with a daily P&L. In my opinion, this is compelling because it provides the agents with direct ownership of their impact on the company. Agents want to know that what they do makes a difference. This allows them to see it clearly."

"We provide timely and pertinent performance feedback."

"We have had success with better and more focused feedback to the staff about Performance (contact monitoring and evaluations)."

"We set explicit and measurable performance plans that included 75% training (computer, office protocols, team building, etc)."

"We became more focused on monthly individual rep dialogues regarding monthly production and quality. We provided immediate contact statistics information to reps each day."

"We provided frequent feedback on agents' performance and contributions."

"We provided an incentive program that is two-tiered. The first level is based on the collector efficiency results (i.e., time on system, number of contacts, promises etc.). The second tier is measured by the end of the month delinquency results for the company's 30-day accounts. While ultimately these accounts are handed off to 24 regional offices, the Collection Center has a direct bearing on the final results. The turnover at our center has thus far (18 months) been minimal. Turnover for employee dissatisfaction is zero."

"Another thing we do is monitor total contacts for the day, maximum wait times, abandoned contacts, etc. We look at all the statistics. We try to catch our employees "doing something right." We always try to praise them for anything that goes well, to assure them that they know they are appreciated for the day-to-day excellent customer service they give. A major complaint in most contact centers is that they only hear when something is done wrong, but never about all the day-to-day right things they do."

"My best results have come from a combination of communicating expectations, being flexible on coaching techniques, providing honest and positive feedback on a regular basis, not profiling the reps (treating each person with respect and not lumping them all into a single category), and adherence to guidelines (rules)."

"Quarterly I meet individually with the representatives, to go over their performance. This performance is tied directly to their quarterly performance standard incentive. I also provide a weekly e-mail of our contact stats and make sure to praise them for meeting goals. I feel it is also very important that the manager take the time to get out on the floor weekly and speak to the representatives. They appreciate it a lot."

"First and foremost, provide good training. Motivate and encourage phone reps as much as possible. Assure each representative that we are in this together."

"A policy was instituted to give a bead to put on a string whenever anyone gave you feedback (either do more, the same or less) on a behavior. At first it appeared childish, but it then became a serious method for people to communicate and discuss issues that they might not otherwise bring up. Problems didn't build up and expectations were clear."

"We instituted regularly scheduled feedback sessions where observations, review of contact documentation, review of actual contacts and general performance review are discussed. This also gives the CSR a regular time to bring up issues and concerns and discuss ways to improve the process. They feel like they are part of a team that cares about them and their input."

"We monitor contacts heavily and found that the more positive feedback we give to our staff, the happier they are. It seems to have had a definite impact on our turnover. We also make the staff aware of where we are performance wise and solicit their input as to how we can improve. Making the CSR's feel a part of the team has also been a big help. If you show that you appreciate their hard work they seem to want to work harder and go the extra mile to serve our customers."

"We created a measurement tool (productivity) followed by a reward program. This made the staff feel like hard work was rewarded. This creates turnover in the short term but you only lose the people who feel they can't keep up with the average."

"I submit the following criteria for reducing turnover: Keep the work environment positive and upbeat. Establish fair and realistic goals. Conduct regular, open communications meetings. Provide an incentive program based on meeting the goals for both the employee and company."

"We meet with each agent once a month to go over performance objectives. This time is used for one-on-one interaction and allows them to ask questions, receive feedback, give feedback, etc."

"I do several things in my contact center for the staff like keeping them involved in their production by providing them with feedback on the number of contacts they take, talk time and abandoned contacts. The one thing that the staff enjoys the most, which has created a friendly competition with the staff, is I have a "speed demon" award for them. This is a toy red sports car that they get to set on top of their monitor if they have the best talk time for the previous week. In addition to this I have a "slow poke" award, which is a toy pocket scooter that sits on top of the monitor of the person with the longest talk time. This is also awarded weekly. They are all excited about the awards each week to see who it will pass to. They all work hard to try and keep the sports car as long as they can and to get rid of the scooter! As simple as it may seem, it really makes for a good team-building tool while encouraging and rewarding the representatives with the pride of having the car on their desk for the week. They all work harder to avoid getting the scooter, which boosts our production, too."

"The biggest impact on turnover reduction and morale boosting comes from establishing both a career path and a solid bonus structure. Giving people these objectives and goals places responsibility for their career solely on their shoulders. Essentially they were in control of what happens."

"There is no single, unique, compelling reason for reducing turnover. When taking on the assignment of developing and implementing an auto-dialer (collections) for this company, my immediate challenge was to add to staff and then train both the current collectors (who were fairly set in their collection ways) and the new hires. I was already aware of the 'horror' stories concerning the high turnover of personnel in the auto-dialer environment. I made this my "first" priority: keep unwanted turnover at a minimum. The first and best way is to ensure the work environment is positive and upbeat, even when collection results are difficult. Sub-prime collections in today's economic environment are probably as difficult a collection assignment as anybody can imagine. Second on my list was to establish both fair and realistic work standards. Nothing is more de-motivating than having goals that cannot be met."

"The purpose of the program is to build a work environment that allows employees to accomplish their goals and be fulfilled in their work. This is achieved through a process of feedback that promotes a dialog between managers and staff so that action is taken to ensure that employees: know what is expected of them at work; have the tools and materials they need to do their jobs right; receive recognition for doing good work; have their voices heard; are involved in decision making; and can learn, grow, and fulfill their career goals within the company."

"There is no initiative or magic bullet—it's about the basics— make it a place where people want to work:

1. Coaching and follow through - are you helping them grow? Do they know what is expected of them?

2. Consistency and fairness - are people treated equally and with respect?

3. Is the work place a place where you would want to be every day? What about ergonomics, conveniences, social activities?"

"The motivation, compensation and incentive scheme is the most effective way to reduce the agent turnover for an outbound sales function contact center. A fair and just evaluation mechanism is the best way."

"Our company has a very strict attendance policy. While there is not a lot that we can do to change the corporate

117

policy, it does have some areas where an employee can make use of options and "loopholes" so to speak. We aggressively educated our employees on both the reasoning behind the policy and how it actually works. That way, they are able to manage their attendance and stay within policy, which prevents mandatory terminations for attendance policy violations."

4. Investing in CSRs/Training

"Our best solution to agent turnover was our offer of benefits coupled with education reimbursements. The offer to have a comprehensive medical and benefit package available to all employees helped our contact center significantly reduce turnover over a period of time. We also offered an education reimbursement package with limits per year for complete reimbursement for the employee's college education. The yearly limit on the expenditure allowed the employees to complete their college degree within a six-year period. Agents knew that if they left the company, they would have to pay on their own; this kept the employee on the job for at least six years. I'm not sure of the financial impact, but agent turnover was significantly reduced. Another situation that worked, which I have seen, is that of an employer with outstanding benefits, and a split of 20% employer workforce and 80% outsourced staffing. The outsourced staffing would be at the site 10 to15 years waiting for the chance to become a full time employee of the company. Turnover in this case was less than 5%."

"It made the agents more productive as they could handle more contacts. It made their jobs more interesting as they handled a greater variety of contacts. They tend to stay longer because they are not in a dead-end position. I am able to justify increases because of their total added value to the company."

"We implemented a new extended training program that has three modules. This gives the employee time to acclimate to the surroundings and have time to concentrate on smaller bits of information at a time. We also have developed training to promote our clients and all the good they do. The employees like this because they feel good about what they are doing."

"In our customer service department, we created the Career Institute, with very clear paths of promotional and lateral opportunities for our customer service representatives. We met with each CSR individually to identify which path best met their interests and abilities. Our skills development program has enabled us to fill most positions internally, which has had the greatest effect on retaining our best associates. The Career Institute has had a positive ripple effect throughout our contact center, as associates see their colleagues reaching their professional goals, and many are setting similar goals. Retention has increased dramatically since this program launched one year ago."

"We instituted a training and certification program geared around general technology (i.e., computer operating systems, LAN/WAN concepts) and the products that we support (proprietary PC and Internet-based software). We made the certification program modular and tied advancement from first level to second level (and the associated raises) into the certification program as well as a requirement for special assignments."

"In a customer service organization, you must try to expand the scope of the work of the agent, and as a consequence add more value to the customer."

"A career path lets the CSR grow within the organization as well as other positions outside the contact center. We set up an internship-like program for contact center representatives going to school for things like marketing, finance etc. Some moved into those positions for the company and the contact center became a feeder pool for the organization."

"One of our most successful techniques was the establishment of a career ladder for CSRs that not only includes career development in our contact center, but also extended into other positions in the company, including Training, Contracts Administration and Credit/Collections."

"The implementation of cross-functional teams worked wonders for us. Agents were scheduled to work in areas other than the contact center, i.e., on site support, documentation, etc. Training! Agents want to know the latest and greatest technologies. Getting the agents involved in off-phone subject-matter-expert type work is a sure-fire success tool. This allows them to see the organization at a different level. It increases buy-in and they feel closer to the work and believe they have more control over what they do."

"If they are well trained and up-to-date, they are not bored."

A CSR Certification programs, linked with compensation and achievement of objectives, was well received in our center.

"We expanded duties and knowledge to allow agents to succeed and feel successful in delivering one-stop quality service."

"We have replaced monetary incentives with employee-focused activities. We have made a concerted effort to develop the whole employee rather than just the person we see at work. One thing that has been very successful for us is incorporating a certified therapist in our training sessions. The training is attended by each team as a team. Changes, procedures, etc. are taught half the day and the other half is dedicated to personal development. Stress management, personalities and "how to handle differences" are a few of the topics discussed. We plan to keep this as an ongoing part of training."

"Providing professional and knowledge growth possibilities through training and modification of duties and including the individuals in the decisions regarding their particular direction (for training and for new duties) works for us."

"I noticed the best impact on turnover when I implemented a clear short-term career opportunity: a special group of agents to handle escalated contacts before they went to a supervisor. That group was called the Customer Care Group. Those agents received fifty cents more an hour and were respected and envied by the other agents. The whole floor then tried to get into that group. I had lower turnover and many agents exerted extra effort."

"Prospective agents need to be fully apprised of job requirements with its positive and negative ramifications. If they are, and then they are rigorously trained, basically receiving a complete exposure of what they can expect to encounter in the day-to-day functions of the position, the overall attrition rate is definitely minimized. This approach will definitely negatively impact the number of trainees who accept the position, but the approach works to cut down on people who leave."

"I don't know that our solution is necessarily unique, however, we have combined some things and we have seen results. We improved our training. We have put levels in place so that a representative can progress once additional training has been had. We added an incentive program tied to business objectives, and we added part-time opportunities. We still see some turnover, but usually this is to other departments in the organization."

'Training and compensation are the two main issues we deal with on ongoing basis. Training has given the employees the confidence they need to help the members. In the three years that I have been in the contact center, most of my turnover has been due to promotions to other departments."

"Career pathing has been a big help for us. We have given emphasis on improving compensation and clear advancement opportunities for our reps. They see the investment and realize they have just as good of an opportunity here as anywhere else."

"Our center implemented an employee retention plan last year increasing salaries and monthly incentives. We also extended our training program to six weeks. The combination of the two has decreased our turnover."

"Creating a career path and opportunities for growth and career development for the help desk agents made a difference for us. The second most important initiative is providing and paying for additional training and classes. The

121

third most important is involving the help desk in the development process and other projects that impact the help desk."

"In conjunction with my supervisory staff, we developed and implemented a career path in a contact center that did not have ANY chance for advancement. We have continued to develop and enhance the career path to include additional levels as well as entry-level-exempt staff positions. Unfortunately, many of our staff still leave for better-paying positions. We are located in a very competitive market for experienced (which they get from us) contact center agents."

"Providing a career path for the agents within your own organization is the number one way of retaining good agents. Career development plans are discussed at each appraisal period and documented with specific on the job or classroom experiences deemed necessary to enhance the agent's value."

"Techniques and processes that worked for us are empowerment of agents, employee participation in contact center changes and strategies, cross-training opportunities with our operations area and a revamped coaching system."

Better training

"We provided advanced training on customer service, relationship building, sales, etc. We including CSRs in planning and implementation of service/contact center initiatives."

"We provided career progression opportunities within the department, for example, writing reports and creating presentations."

"We introduced incentives and rewards as well as improved training. Another aspect, which may have helped, is the introduction of smart casual attire instead of business attire."

"Definitely, offering increased training was a plus. A survey of agents, the increased training opportunities showed that management was interested in the staff's growth and would offer advancement."

"The position was re-evaluated and re-leveled. We have also put into place a very structured training program."

"We set explicit, measurable performance plans that included 75% training (computer, office protocols, team building, etc.)."

"We initiated a praise in public program. Each agent earns 15 minutes to use at their discretion within the next quarter. It can be accumulated or taken as earned. Each representative that earns time receives a large sign/plaque to be hung in their cubicle. This lets everyone know who is producing and who is not. Cash incentives are not something we are currently offering, but we do give gift cards also for the store of their choice on a monthly basis if they exceed their performance goals. It is important to reward and praise each representative individually. Treating them as adults will only push them to strive higher and stick with the company. We are a major servicer in the mortgage industry, and our representatives are consistently on a contact campaign (inbound/outbound). Our corporation offers many benefits to help them grow professionally while encouraging growth. Tuition assistance is one benefit that many take advantage of."

"One year ago, I inherited a contact center with over 40% annual turnover. One year later we are running about 10 to 15% max. Those that do attempt to leave for favorable reason undergo possible conversion from full-time to part-time. There were several key items that influenced this in order of most significant. 1) We changed hiring practice to include at least two years of contact center experience before representative was interviewed/hired. The primary reason was to have a group of individuals that understand basics of contact center 101 and stress etc., as well as reduced transient contact center behavior (reps moving from one center to collect sign on bonuses or continual paid training). 2) We initiated and benchmarked tele-skills test from a local labor agency to determine customer service skills and keyboard operation. We calibrated tests at the top 50% skill level. 3) We initiated an environment/philosophy of organize, train and equip department. This overall philosophy reduced anxiety in planning, increased awareness to take care of those

123

things that allow representatives to do their jobs, resulting in fairness and associate satisfaction with management team."

"First and foremost, we provide good training. We motivate and encourage phone reps as much as possible. We ensure each representative that we are in this together. We try to be consistent on policies and procedures."

"We provide in depth training to answer a broader scope of questions."

"We increased the scope of our education and training. That had the biggest effect on reducing our turnover."

"We had success with salary increases and empowering employees by allowing them to assist in selecting their schedule and training."

"Two powerful motivators in our shop have been the opportunity for promotion and more training."

"We created a very positive work environment by providing training that reduces mistakes and therefore maximizes the chance for a bonus."

"Because we are supporting a fixed-price government contract, there are limitations to what we can do in the areas of compensation and training. We focused on internal appreciation programs for our agents. Specifically, we instituted an 'Agent of the Month' award. The winner's picture was published in the base newspaper. The winner also received little things like a free lunch with the boss. We also established a 'kudos' program (an on-the-spot award that any customer or staff member could make) and some cross training and mentoring and schedule rotation of the teams (i.e., desktop support would work with network support for a day, etc.)."

"Introducing fun and making the day easier to get through when it has been especially challenging has been helpful in our center. We also made a lot of points by increasing the pay rate and offering training."

5. Belonging/Fun Place to Work/Part of the Team

"It's not all about pay - it's about creating an environment where the employee feels valued and part of a community."

"We're located in the metropolitan D.C. area, and found that salary and location play a key role in attracting employees. We have trouble attracting employees because we aren't convenient to public transportation. However, those employees who stay with us, do so because of the work environment. We offer a casual work place, flexible schedules and consistent non-dollar rewards. Several employees have moved from retail stores to our contact center and stress that the set schedules and relaxed atmosphere make them happy to come to work."

"The ability to recognize agents' accomplishments combined with building a family environment has worked for us."

"Agents are more likely to stay if they are accepted by the long time guys."

"As the hiring manager's interview skills have developed, we have seen a reduction in turnover and improved morale. Beyond that we have become creative with incentives and promotions. For example, we have created incentives where a supervisor will do your job for an hour or incentives where reps can earn casual wear time."

"Approximately two years ago, our CEO allowed the implementation of an initiative within our contact center that we believe is unique. To combat 50% annual turnover in a tight Atlanta job market, we took the step of reducing the workweek of contact center employees from 40 to 30 hours with the same pay! We now have less than 5% annual negative attrition and no problems attracting new job applicants. In addition, the experience level, job satisfaction and reduction in job stress for our reps have all been impacted positively. The savings of no longer having to constantly replace reps has offset the budgetary costs of increasing our staff to make up for the hours of converting to a 30-hour workweek."

"We try to really promote a family atmosphere and flexible scheduling (for schooling and family activities). We are a small contact center, so we do a rotating shift where they work 7:30 to 5 Monday through Thursday and 8 to 2 on Friday (no lunch). They really enjoy being off for half of the day. As we anticipate growing, we are hoping to go to four 10-hour days or something creative with 9-hour shifts. We are initiating activities that recognize the level of support the Customer Service Representative is giving our customers."

"We believe in creating a fun, yet productive work environment."

"We are building trust with the staff- at all levels. It's not something that happens over night, but by having regularly scheduled communication briefings (45 to- 60 minutes) of small-ish groups (15 to 20)) of all levels of staff, you can give them lots of information, as well as address the "rumor mill" and other questions. This, as well as having a weekly communication vehicle, like a newsletter, that contains column(s) by top management, reduces an "us vs. them" situation, by letting even the most junior staff feel they are privy to most, or all, of the same information as everyone else. No one can play "lord" over another person just because they know something that the other person does not. Communication is very vital to instilling trust and comfort amongst the staff."

"Our best results came from focusing on smaller team sizes and providing more access to the supervisor."

"First of all there really is no one thing that is a magic pill for turnover, but a number of small things that make a big difference. You must be committed to making your work environment a place people want to come into and succeed. If I were to site one thing which does stand out above the others it would be to model the behaviors of your representatives you would deem to be successful and go and advertise and look for those qualities. Too many people advertise generically and weed through them to try to find the minimum characteristics needed. Focus your search on the successful agent model and go find them."

"Based on their skills, agents may be involved in planning stages and interact face to face with the client. This will provide the agent with deeper understanding of the business it is going to interact with."

"I do several things in my contact center for the staff like keeping them involved in their production by providing them with feedback on the number of contacts they take, talk time and abandoned contacts. The one thing that the staff enjoys the most, which has created a friendly competition with the staff, is I have a "speed demon" award for them. This is a toy red sports car that they get to set on top of their monitor if they have the best talk time for the previous week. In addition to this I have a "slow poke" award, which is a toy pocket scooter that sits on top of the monitor of the person with the longest talk time. This is also awarded weekly. They are all excited about the awards each week to see who it will pass to. They all work hard to try and keep the sports car as long as they can and to get rid of the scooter! As simple as it may seem, it really makes for a good team-building tool while encouraging and rewarding the representatives with the pride of having the car on their desk for the week. They all work harder to avoid getting the scooter, which boosts our production, too."

"We really don't have undue turnover for the size of our center. We do, however, use the "Fish" philosophy in having fun at work."

"This is no single unique and compelling reason for reducing turnover. When taking on the assignment of developing and implementing an auto-dialer (collections) to this company, my immediate challenge was to add to staff and then train both the current collectors (who were fairly set in their collection ways) and the new hires. I was already aware of the "horror" stories concerning the high turnover of personnel in the auto-dialer environment. I made this my "first" priority - keep unwanted turnover at a minimum. The first and best way is to ensure the work environment is positive and upbeat, even when collection results are difficult. Sub-prime collections in today's economic environment are probably as difficult a collection assignment as anybody can imagine. Second on my

127

list was to establish both fair and realistic work standards. Nothing is more de-motivating than having goals that cannot be met."

"We have given time off as a reward or prize for hard work. We have been doing fun things at our meetings, such as musical chairs. We have just implemented a new organization structure in our contact center, by adding Team Managers. This helps the reps have someone to go to at all times."

"We started with goals (not stretch) that appeared reasonable. The employees were advised that the goals are not final but only a start. In order to meet the company goals we must do better but that we needed to build some history and measure some results. The goals were subsequently increased several times with minimal objections by the collection staff, including those who had difficulty making their goals. Each time the bar was raised so were the results. The success of raising the goals in a rather short period of time was a direct result of conducting regular and open communications/training meetings. These meetings are held twice a month (always on Friday - it is the lightest day for customer contacts). Refreshments are served and occasionally door prizes are given out. The meetings are scheduled for 30 minutes and are kept to that time limit with rare exception."

"As a summary, I would submit the following criteria for reducing turnover:

1. Keep work environment positive and upbeat.
2. Establish fair and realistic goals.
3. Conduct regular and "open" communications meetings.
4. Provide an incentive program based on meeting the goals for both the employee and company."

"Communication and participation are the best methods to assist in reducing agent attrition. I have implemented a program whereby the business plan for the coming 18 months is personally communicated to each agent (over 50 agents) in groups of 4 and seek their input and feedback. This allows them to better understand who and where the company is heading and therefore they are more committed to their role and where they see they add value to the overall strategy. Also, we introduced the Managers Challenge whereby the agents are provided with a theme to decorate the center or come up with a catch phrase that mirrors the morale and psyche of the center. We involve them in lead generation programs with a reward structure."

"Having a fun atmosphere works for our call center."

"Clear and simple goals, recognition, discipline, communication, birthday cards, friendly competition, strong leadership, quality feedback, pot-lucks, raises in a timely fashion, coaching, delegation and showing career progression are just a few of the keys to building a positive work environment."

"First and foremost, provide good training. Motivate and encourage phone reps as much as possible. Ensure each representative "we are in this together." Be consistent on policies and procedures."

"We achieved positive results by providing career opportunities to top performers for advancement in both their job title and pay, by providing recognition to the entire contact center when department goals are met, and by rewarding top CSR's with incentives. We have created a fun environment to work in."

"The average age in our technical helpdesk contact center (250 seats) is 20 years old. We just make it a fun environment, have parties, nice incentives (movie vouchers, drinks, t-shirts) and we are very flexible in working hours and desk environment. We listen to them and use their ideas to improve their working environment as well as the way we handle customers."

"In state government, the salary level is "the pits." I try to make the work environment fun and rewarding to compensate for the poor salary."

"Making the job fun is difficult, however, we try to have bi-weekly department meetings and do fun activities, along with other team build exercises."

"We started a monthly attendance bonus and also increased our employee referral bonus. It seemed if we hired their friends then not only would both have good attendance but also they would try to compete with each other thus working much harder."

"I would say that it is a combination of things. You need to make the job as fun as possible, listen and invite feedback from associates to get their buy-in and a lot of positive feedback."

"There is no initiative or magic bullet - it's about the basics - Make a place where people want to work."

"Coaching and follow through - are you helping them grow? Do they know what is expected of them?"

"We close the business for two days and give each separate team (coach and agents) a team-building event."

"We involve the agents in development and achievement of Company goals. During the process of defining what the initiatives will be for the coming year, we hold brainstorming sessions (with sticky pads to ensure full involvement and anonymity) for ideas. We boil those down to 3 - 5 main initiatives. Once the executive team outlines the annual initiatives for the company, we brainstorm again to identify how our team will be able to affect those initiatives and outline our specific goals for the quarter. This ensures ownership, accountability, and immediate communication of the goals. This makes employees at all levels feel like they have a part in the direction and decision making of the company."

"Create an employee recognition program, where employees can nominate employees for any job well done. The reward can be as simple as a balloon and a candy bar. Also, we have found that laying out a career path greatly reduces the likelihood of employees leaving the company. Mangers need to take the time to have career development with each of their employees."

"We started batch hiring (more than one person hired and trained as a group) as opposed to individual hiring and training separately. This training was also beefed up with the operations manager participating daily for at least 15 minutes of the training. Retention of this group was 100%."

6. Chance for Advancement

"A career path lets the CSR grow within the organization and prepare for other positions outside the contact center. We set up an internship like program for contact center representatives going to school for things like marketing, finance etc. Some moved into those positions for the company and the contact center became a feeder pool for the organization."

"I noticed the best impact on turnover when I implemented a clear short-term career opportunity. We developed a special group of agents to handle escalated contacts before they went to a supervisor. That group was contacted the Customer Care Group. Those agents received $.50 more per hour and were respected and envied by the other agents. The whole floor then tried to get into that group. I had lower turnover and many agents exerted extra effort."

"Our most compelling initiative involved establishing a career ladder for CSRs that not only included career development in our contact center, but also extended into other positions in the company, including Training, Contracts Administration and Credit/Collections."

"An established career path with accurate documentation that is properly communicated and administered from all aspects of the management team is a necessary tool for agent retention. Agents need to see a "light" at the end of the tunnel and must have a "trail" to get there. Motivation for agents lies in and upon themselves for their own personal reward psyche. Wages, respect and satisfaction are necessary for people to believe and stay with an organization."

"We created a career path and opportunities for growth and career development for the help desk agents. The second most important initiative is providing and paying for additional training and classes. The third most important is involving the help desk in the development process and other projects that impact the help desk. In our customer service department, we created the Career Institute, with very clear paths of promotional and lateral opportunities for our customer service representatives. We met with each CSR individually to identify which path best met their interests and abilities. Our skills development program has enabled us to fill most positions internally, which has had the greatest effect on retaining our best associates. The Career Institute has had a positive ripple effect throughout our contact center, as associates see their colleagues reaching their professional goals, and many are setting similar goals. Retention has increased dramatically since this program launched one year ago."

"Career pathing has been a big help for us. We have given emphasis on improving compensation and clear advancement opportunities for our reps. They see the investment and realize they have just as good of an opportunity here as anywhere else."

"We instituted a training and certification program geared around general technology (i.e., computer operating systems, LAN/WAN concepts) and the products that we support (proprietary PC and Internet based software). We made the certification program modular and tied advancement from first level to second level (and the associated raises) into the certification program as well as a requirement for special assignments."

"We initiated a CSR Certification programs, linked with compensation and achievement of objectives."

"Something that helped our center was the recent promotion of some of my contact center agents to positions within the company, which shows that there is a light at the end of the contact center tunnel."

"We expanded duties and knowledge to allow agents to succeed and feel successful in delivering one-stop quality service."

"We implemented a Quality of Worklife Program. The purpose of the program is to build a work environment that allows employees to accomplish their goals and be fulfilled in their work. This is achieved through a process of feedback that promotes a dialog between managers and staff so that action is taken to ensure that employees:

- know what is expected of them at work
- have the tools and materials they need to do their jobs right
- receive recognition for doing good work
- have their voices heard, and are involved in decision making
- can learn, grow, and fulfill their career goals within the company."

"We developed and implemented a career path in a contact center that did not have any chance for advancement. We have continued to develop and enhance the career path to include additional levels as well as entry-level exempt staff positions. Unfortunately, many of our staff still leave for better paying positions. We are located in a very competitive market for experienced (which they get from us) contact center agents."

"We discuss career development plans are discussed at each appraisal period and documented with specific on the job or classroom experiences deemed necessary to enhance the agent's value."

"We made great strides by providing career opportunities to top performers for advancement in both their job title and pay, by providing recognition to the entire contact center when department goals are met, and by rewarding top CSRs with incentives. Lastly, we created a fun creating a fun environment to work in."

"Our contact center went to skill base routing. This has provided a ladder for growth and an avenue for additional compensation."

"When I began as Contact Center Manager, our turnover rate was over 50%. I found the primary reason for leaving was frustration and lack of opportunity. The agents did not understand the basics of how a contact center works or even their purpose for doing what they do. We put together a 4-hour training program that greatly helped. In addition we put together a career pathing initiative."

"Career pathing and skill-based pay worked wonders for us. We reward agents through salary increases once they have attained and mastered certain skill sets."

"We providing more discretionary decision-making responsibility to staff integrated with a visible career path."

"The opportunity for promotion and training proved to be a powerful motivator."

"Clear and simple goals, recognition, discipline, communication, birthday cards, friendly competition, strong leadership, quality feedback, pot-lucks, raises in a timely fashion, coaching, delegation and showing career progression are just a few of the keys to success with retention."

"We suggest developing a clear path for advancement in responsibilities and compensation."

"I don't know that our solution is necessarily unique, however, we have combined some things and seen results. We have increased and improved our training. We have put levels in place so that a representative can progress once additional training is in place. We have added an incentive program tied to business objectives. We have added part-time opportunities. We still see some turnover, but usually this is to other departments in the organization."

"We provided career progression opportunities within the department, for example, writing reports and creating presentations."

"Establishing a career path and a solid bonus structure seemed to make the biggest impact on turnover reduction and morale. Giving people these objectives and goals place the responsibility of their future/career solely on their shoulders. Then they are in control of what happens."

"Definitely a primary initiative is offering increased training. In a survey of agents, the increased training opportunities showed that management was interested in the staff's growth and would offer advancement."

"Create an employee recognition program, where employees can nominate employees for any job well done. The reward can be as simple as a balloon and a candy bar. Also, we have found that laying out a career path greatly reduces the likelihood of employees leaving the company. Mangers need to take the time to have career development with each of their employees."

7. Effective Communication

"Building trust with the staff at all levels is essential. It's not something that happens over night, but by having regularly scheduled communication briefings (45-60 minutes) of small-ish groups (15-20 max) of all levels of staff, you can give them lots of information, as well as address the "rumor mill" and other questions. This, as well as having a weekly communication vehicle, like a newsletter, that contains column(s) by top management, reduces an "us vs. them" situation, by letting even the most junior staff feel they are privy to most, or all, of the same information as everyone else. No one can play "lord" over another person just because they know something that the other person does not. Communication is very vital to instilling trust and comfort amongst the staff."

"Becoming more focused on monthly individual rep dialogues regarding monthly production and quality, and providing immediate contact statistics information to reps each day helped our center."

"We started with goals (not stretch) that appeared reasonable. The employees were advised that the goals are not final but only a start. In order to meet the company goals we must do better but that we needed to build some history and measure some results. The goals were subsequently increased several times with minimal objections by the collection staff, including those who had difficulty making their goals. Each time the bar was raised so were the results.

The success of raising the goals in a rather short period of time was a direct result of conducting regular and open communications/training meetings. These meetings are held twice a month (always on Friday - it is the lightest day for customer contacts). Refreshments are served and occasionally door prizes are given out. They meetings are scheduled for 30 minutes and are kept to that time limit with rare exception."

"Communication and participation are the best methods to assist in reducing agent attrition. I have implemented a program whereby the business plan for the coming 18 months is personally communicated to each agent (over 50 agents) in groups of 4 and seek their input and feedback. This allows them to better understand who and where the company is heading and therefore they are more committed to their role and where they see they add value to the overall strategy. Also, introducing the Managers Challenge whereby the agents are provided with a theme to decorate the center or come up with a catch phrase that mirrors the morale and psyche of the center. We like to involve agents in a lead generation program with a reward structure."

"Introduction of the SITEL Management System (SMS) which enabled us to share agent performance data in a real-time basis, twice a day, was a major boost to our center."

"We involved the agents in the development and achievement of company goals. During the process of defining what the initiatives will be for the coming year, we hold brainstorming sessions (with sticky pads to ensure full involvement and anonymity) for ideas. We boil those down to 3 to 5 main initiatives. Once the executive team outlines the annual initiatives for the company, we brainstorm again to identify how our team will be able to affect those initiatives and outline our specific goals for the quarter. This ensures ownership, accountability, and immediate communication of the goals. This makes employees at all levels feel like they have a part in the direction and decision making of the company."

"In addition, we meet with each agent once per month to go over performance objectives. Also, this time is used for one-on-one interaction, allowing them to ask questions, receive feedback, give feedback, etc."

"We instituted regularly scheduled feedback sessions where observations, review of contact documentation, review of actual contacts and general performance review are discussed. This also gives the CSR a regular time to bring up issues and concerns and discuss ways to improve the process. They feel like they are part of a team that cares about them and their input."

"I believe that communicating the corporate philosophy and providing employee development and career opportunities and advancement and actually executing these progressive ideas has been the greatest impact to reducing attrition."

"We also did skip level meetings once a month. This was a meeting with the representatives (supervisors were skipped) and the contact center to share information. We also created an advisory committee that helped our management solve the tough issues."

"Every two weeks all Contact Center employees fill out a survey. If scores are low, we can see the warning signs early and try to give individuals extra attention, and may change process/procedures as a result of the feedback. It's worked great."

"We provide regular meetings with the General Manager."

"We promote an inclusive management and leadership style. We have focused on development of a team approach to contact center operations."

"Focusing on smaller team sizes and providing more access to the supervision helps a lot."

"We provide frequent feedback on agents' performance and contributions."

"We decided to help curb turnover in two easy ways. The first thing we did was scratch our old interview process and put more time and energy in to the new process. We felt that giving the candidates the most "true view" of our Contact

Center would educate them in making a long-term commitment. We now involve peer interviews all the way to a face-to-face with the VP. So far, the turnover rate has decreased slightly, but with tons of potential. The second initiative also involved scratching an old process with a new one. Our previous Orientation program typically lasted about two hours. Our new and improved (and very informative) Orientation lasts at least three days. We give new employees a view of the whole company and how it works, rather than just an overview of their department. This, plus the above mentioned have shown potential to greatly reduce turnover."

"We show appreciation to the staff. We monitor contacts heavily and found that the more positive feedback we give to our staff the happier they are. It seems to have had a definite impact on our turnover. We also make the staff aware of where we are performance wise and solicit their input as to how we can improve. Making the CSRs feel a part of the team has also been a big help. If you show that you appreciate their hard work they seem to want to work harder and go the extra mile to serve our customers."

"As a summary, I would submit the following criteria for reducing turnover:

1. Keep work environment positive and upbeat

2. Establish fair and realistic goals

3. Conduct regular and "open" communications meetings

4. Provide an incentive program based on meeting the goals for both the employee and company."

"Empowerment of agents, employee participation in contact center changes and strategies, cross-training opportunities with our operations area and a revamped coaching system have had a positive impact."

"We implemented a Quality of Worklife Program. The purpose of the program is to build a work environment that allows employees to accomplish their goals and be fulfilled in their work. This is achieved through a process of feedback that promotes a dialog between managers and staff so that action is taken to ensure that employees:

- know what is expected of them at work
- have the tools and materials they need to do their jobs right
- receive recognition for doing good work
- have their voices heard, and are involved in decision making
- can learn, grow, and fulfill their career goals within the company."

"We believe that providing a career path for the agents within your own organization is the number one way of retaining good agents. Career development plans are discussed at each appraisal period and documented with specific on the job or classroom experiences deemed necessary to enhance the agent's value."

"Our company has a very strict attendance policy. While there is not a lot that we can do to change the corporate policy, it does have some areas where an employee can make use of options and loopholes so to speak. We very aggressively educated our employees on both the reasoning behind the policy and how it actually works. That way, they are able to manage their attendance and stay within policy, which prevents mandatory terminations for attendance policy violations."

"Opening the doors of communication and teamwork to all levels of support is a priority of ours."

"Feedback is very crucial. I meet with the representatives individually, quarterly, to go over their performance. This performance is tied directly to their quarterly performance standard incentive. I also provide a weekly e-mail of our contact stats and make sure to praise them for meeting goals. I feel it is also very important that the manager take the time to get out on the floor weekly and speak to the representatives, they appreciate it a lot."

"When I began as Contact Center Manager, our turnover rate was over 50%. I found the primary reason for leaving was frustration and lack of opportunity. The agents did not understand the basics of how a contact center works or even their purpose for doing what they do. We put together a 4-hour training program that greatly helped. In addition we put together a career pathing initiative."

"Making the job fun is difficult, however, we try to have bi-weekly department meetings and do fun activities, along with other team building exercises."

"I would say that it is a combination of things. You need to make the job as fun as possible, listen and invite feedback from associates to get their buy-in and a lot of positive feedback."

8. Performance Based Incentives

"We implemented a Customer Satisfaction incentive bonus plan allowing for increasing bonuses year after year based on customer satisfaction achievement levels. Based on customer satisfaction performance, an employee can earn 5K after one year, 10K after 2 years, 15K after 3 years and 20K after 4 years. Performance that is rewarded against corporate customer satisfaction goals, but the stepped up bonus amounts have inherent retention incentive. Costs are justified by reduced cost of turnover, productivity gains of having more experienced agents, and long-term profitability of corporation through improved customer satisfaction and loyalty. Plan has reduced turnover from 31% to 17%."

"The motivation compensation and incentive scheme is the most effective way to reduce the agent turnover for the outbound sales function contact center."

"We have developed a variable incentive program for our agents that allows them to generate significant earnings, beyond what they would normally command in the marketplace. At the same time I have driven my acquisition unit costs down to world-class levels as a result of increased productivity."

"Feedback is very crucial. I meet with the representatives individually, quarterly, to go over their performance. This performance is tied directly to their quarterly performance standard incentive. I also provide a weekly e-mail of our contact stats and make sure to praise them for meeting goals.

I feel it is also very important that the manager take the time to get out on the floor weekly and speak to the representatives, they appreciate it a lot."

"By providing career opportunities to top performers for advancement in both their job title and pay, by providing recognition to the entire contact center when department goals are met, and by rewarding top CSRs with incentives. Lastly, by creating a fun environment to work in."

9. Merit/productivity-based pay

"Our center implemented an employee retention plan last year increasing salaries and monthly incentives. We also extended our training program to 6 weeks. The combination of the two has decreased our turnover."

"Productivity and quality-linked incentives that are meaningful are invaluable."

"We have incentive programs, that inspire pride and a sense of ownership."

"We created a measurement tool (productivity) followed by a reward program. This made staff feel like hard work was rewarded. This creates turnover in the short term but you only loss the staff that doesn't feel they can keep up with the average."

"We have incentives tied to performance. We recognize individual accomplishments and praise and reward for going the extra mile."

"I don't know that our solution is necessarily unique, however, we have combined some things and seen results. We have increased and improved our training. We have put levels in place so that a representative can progress once additional training is in place. We have added an incentive program tied to business objectives. We have added part-time opportunities. We still see some turnover, but usually this is to other departments in the organization."

Compensation incentives

"Our program includes providing training that reduces mistakes and therefore maximizes the chance for a bonus combined with creating a very positive work environment."

"We have provided an incentive program that is two-tiered. The first level is based on the collector efficiency results (i.e., Time on System, Number of Contacts, Promises etc.). The second tier is measured by the end-of-the-month delinquency results for the company's 30-day accounts. While ultimately these accounts are handed off to 24 regional offices, the Collection Center has a direct bearing on the final results. The turnover at our center has thus far (18 months) been minimal. Turnover for employee dissatisfaction is zero."

"As a summary, I would submit the following criteria for reducing turnover:

1. Keep work environment positive and upbeat.

2. Establish fair and realistic goals.

3. Conduct regular and "open" communications meetings.

4. Provide an incentive program based on meeting the goals for both the employee and company."

"We introduced incentives and rewards as well as improved training. Another aspect, which may have helped, is the introduction of smart casual attire instead of business attire."

"Establishing a Career Path and a solid bonus structure seemed to make the biggest impact on turnover reduction and morale. Giving people these objectives and goals place the responsibility of their future/career solely on their shoulders. They control what happens."

"Pay for performance seemed to help a bit, but we still have turnover from employees returning to school/college."

"We promote praise in public. Each agent earns 15 minutes to use at their discretion within the next quarter. It can be accumulated or taken as earned. Each representative that earns time receives a large sign/plaque to be hung in their cubicle. This lets everyone know who is producing and who is not. Cash incentives are not something we are currently offering, but we do give gift cards also for the store of their choice on a monthly basis if they exceed their performance goals. It is important to reward and praise each representative individually. Treating them as adults will only push them to strive higher and stick with the company. We are a major servicer in the mortgage industry and our representatives are consistently on a contact campaign (inbound/outbound). Our corporation offers many benefits to help them grow professionally while encouraging self-growth. Tuition assistance is one benefit that many take advantage of."

10. Tools to do the job

"Improvements in technology have helped. By use of computer based "soft phones," the agent is only working with one device. We are also using wireless headsets, which allow the agent to be able to get up and move around from their workstation. This way they can go to the fax or to files and still remain available for a contact or continue with their current contact."

"By providing the best possible tools for agents to do their job contributes to their feeling job satisfaction."

"We are definitely in favor of improved desktop applications. We have implemented and have been refining agent access to customer data. Our business provides numerous types of contracts. Easy and fast access to this data helps our agents provide fast access to information required by our customers."

"We hired a programmer who completely re-wrote the software we were using, which made the intake personnel more comfortable with the process and expedited the contact process. This same programmer utilized a program that integrated our telephone systems with our computer systems, allowing us to identify the client before actually answering the telephone. This also allowed us to access the client's information before the contact process began, affording us the opportunity to review the client information before we had them on the phone."

"We improved desktop technology to make life easier for the staff."

"We executed a change in technology to a much more user-friendly system that was totally integrated with our database that virtually eliminated our agents having to look up customer information. They received an automated screen pop with each incoming contact for all existing customer. System is totally GUI based and easily administered on the fly."

"We had success with empowerment - giving agents the tools and authority to use them."

"Some drawbacks to hiring and retention are: poor tools and multiple systems to use, each with it's own interface, response time and rules of logic. Learning how to use these is time-consuming and frustrating. Seemingly, it takes forever to train and some agents just don't think it is worth it for the entry-level salary."

"We have incorporated integrated software solutions, which reduce the complexity of the CSR's job."

"We expanded duties and knowledge to allow agents to succeed and feel successful in delivering one-stop quality service."

"One year ago, I inherited a contact center with over 40% annual turnover. One year later we are running about 10 to 15% max. Those that do attempt to leave for favorable reasons undergo possible conversion from full-time to part-time. Several key items influenced this. In order of most significant, they are (1) We changed hiring practice to include at least two years of contact center experience before a representative was interviewed/hired. The primary reason was to have a group of individuals that understand the basics of Contact Center 101 and stress etc., as well as reduced transient contact center behavior (reps moving from one center to collect sign on bonuses or continual paid training). (2) We initiated and benchmarked telephone-skills tests from a local labor agency to determine customer service skills and keyboard operation. We calibrated the test at the top 50%

staff skill level. (3) Initiated an environment/philosophy of "organize, train and equip the department. This overall philosophy reduced anxiety in planning and increased awareness to take care of those things that allow representatives to do their jobs resulting in fairness and associate satisfaction with the management team."

"The center I support has been live for four months. We have only had one agent leave at this time and he was clearly a mismatch in talent from early in the process. However we are using the knowledge base for technical support. In addition, we are using the contact recording system to provide opportunities for positive feedback and training opportunities capturing both voice and data information."

"We implemented a Quality of Worklife Program. The purpose of the program is to build a work environment that allows employees to accomplish their goals and be fulfilled in their work. This is achieved through a process of feedback that promotes a dialog between managers and staff so that action is taken to ensure that employees:

- know what is expected of them at work
- have the tools and materials they need to do their jobs right
- receive recognition for doing good work
- have their voices heard, and are involved in decision making
- can learn, grow, and fulfill their career goals within the company."

"We found that better tools to perform job functions leads to a positive mental attitude."

Other/Miscellaneous

Fair Pay

"Introducing fun and making the day easier to get through when it has been especially challenging. Also, increasing the pay rate and offering training worked wonders."

145

"Our center implemented an employee retention plan last year which entailed increasing salaries and offering monthly incentives. We also extended our training program to six weeks. The combination of the two has decreased our turnover."

"We initiated increased compensation coupled with recognition of support role for Help Desk personnel."

"We developed a clear path for advancement in responsibilities and compensation."

"We implemented a Customer Satisfaction incentive bonus plan allowing for increasing bonuses year after year based on customer satisfaction achievement levels. Based on customer satisfaction performance, an employee can earn 5K after one year, 10K after 2 years, 15K after 3 years and 20K after 4 years. Performance that is rewarded against corporate customer satisfaction goals, but the stepped up bonus amounts have inherent retention incentive. Costs are justified by reduced cost of turnover, productivity gains of having more experienced agents, and long-term profitability of corporation through improved customer satisfaction and loyalty. The plan has reduced turnover from 31% to 17%."

Revenue sharing for up selling.

"A few years ago our company was sold to another company. In order to keep as many employees as possible, the new company initiated a stay bonus - one thousand dollars if you were still employed with the company a year after the sale. That year was the lowest turnover we've experienced however after the payout we had a month of the highest turnover ever."

"Our ace in the hole has been salary, which is better than what competitors can offer."

"Considering that we are a 24x7 operation, we lost most of our people to jobs that offered a Monday through Friday schedule. We achieved a reduction in turnover by offering a pay differential for working weekends."

"We found success with Career Pathing and skill-based pay. We also reward agents through salary increases once they have attained and mastered certain skill sets."

"Cross-training! It made the agents more productive as they could handle more contacts. It made their jobs more interesting as they handled a greater variety of contacts. They tend to stay longer because they are not in a dead-end position. I am able to justify increases because of their total added value to the company."

"The most unique and compelling agent turnover reduction initiative was to set up multiple levels within the contact center for career advancement. Moving agents from junior to senior to specialist classes in their title adds value and pride to their position. Each level carries with it a slight pay increase that is more than offset by our improvements in agent retention."

"The position was re-evaluated and re-leveled. We have also put into place a very structured training program."

"We employ a large number of part-time (college students) with very flexible hours. We also offer tuition reimbursement for some classes. Part-time employees who work 50% of their hours after regular bank hours also receive a 10% shift differential. We have very little turnover in our part-time staff."

"This is not unique, but it is compelling: we increased wages by approximately 20% across the board! (They were very low to begin with.)"

"We promote clear and simple goals, recognition, discipline, communication, birthday cards, friendly competition, strong leadership, quality feedback, pot-lucks, raises in a timely fashion, coaching, delegation and showing career progression."

"We linking the value generated to the company by the representative, to the representative's compensation. Coupling that effort with creating a 'professional' sales environment made the difference."

"Work to get the best financial package (i.e., salary, bonus, commission) possible. Most times this is where I fall short. Increased salaries are not easy to come by these days and that can be very un-motivating very quickly."

"Our contact center went to skill base routing. This has provided a ladder for growth and additional compensation."

"In our case, we adjusted the wage rate upward to be similar to our competition in town."

"We offer a bonus program that escalates in amount the longer the agent stays with the campaign. Also, we provide support for a very cool Consumer Electronics product, and if the agent stays a year, he or she is awarded ownership of a unit."

"We found that increase in salary, and empowerment of employees to assist in selecting their schedule and training had a positive impact on our call center."

"A local company implemented a skill-based pay and performance pan about 2 years ago and grandfathered it to their existing associates. If I understand it correctly, associates enter their Contact Center at entry-level salary grade and pay. They have the opportunity to earn more pay based on tenure and performance. The increments of time that they are reviewed and compensated accordingly are 6 months, 12 months and then 18 months. At 18 months, they will have maxed out their pay for their salary grade. All salary increases after that are yearly and based on performance. The average yearly increase is around 4%."

Freedom / Trust to Do the Job

"In the area of agent empowerment, we encourage employee participation in contact center changes and strategies. We provide cross-training opportunities with our operations area and a revamped coaching system."

Value in Internal Organization

"Treat the phone representatives as the most important part of your organization - they are."

"Recognize the CSRs as an integral part of the organization."

"I elevated their salary within the company to a higher level than similar positions in the organization. This has helped keep the turnover down and also brought in more internal applications for new openings."

"We improved our recruiting efforts to better qualify our agents, thus making better hiring decisions. At the same time we also made it harder (increased justification required before hiring additional staff) for other departments to hire members of the support staff."

"The position was re-evaluated and re-leveled. We have also put into place a very structured training program."

"We created a career ladder for our non-technical and technical and healthcare professional agents. This led to increased morale and job satisfaction and gave the agents something to strive for. The 'promotion' to a higher level is based on a number of factors, most notably performance. When agents realize that they have an opportunity to progress within our organization, they are more willing to "dedicate" themselves. We also make the promotion event well known through the whole company."

Variety in the Day (i.e., "Time off the Phones!")

"Give the contact center professional an on-going task unrelated to answering contacts. This gives him/her a break and an opportunity to be creative while working on another project. The project can be assigned by management or suggested by the employee, i.e., recommended telephone procedures, small programming tasks, designing forms, surveying the other staff to get improvement ideas, etc. Additionally, management has a responsibility to reaffirm to the contact center staff their worth to the organization. Management needs to remember these employees hear complaints all day long which can be mentally draining. An occasional pat on the back and understanding ear will go a long way."

"We primarily use part-time staff. The addition of full-time positions that offered health benefits was appealing. Part-time staff prefers working morning schedules. We offered more morning shifts to part-time which enabled our full-time staff to handle off phone responsibilities in the morning."

"We have implemented a policy that allows our agents one hour per day to do work other than answering the phone."

"We provide opportunities for off-phone work projects."

"We implement a varied work schedule with tasks outside of the help desk - project participation, assisting production, etc."

Flexibility / Advocating for CSRs

"Flexible shifts and the possibility of trading unattractive shifts with other agents boosts morale."

"Our contact center is in India and giving the agents ability to rotate shifts was the most significant aspect that led to increased satisfaction, and ultimately, decreased turnover."

"We try to really promote the family atmosphere and flexible scheduling (for schooling and family activities). We are a small contact center, so we do a rotating shift where they work 7:30-5 Monday through Thursday and 8-2 on Friday (no lunch). They really enjoy being off for half of the day. As we anticipate growing, we are hoping to go to four 10-hour days or something creative with 9-hour shifts. Initiating activities that recognize the level of support the Customer Service Representative is giving our customers."

Better flexibility in scheduling

"As a state tax agency we are required to be available to the citizens from 8:00 a.m. to 5:00 p.m. Monday through Friday. Obviously, our busiest time of the year is January through June. We have reviewed our incoming contacts and the times those contacts come in. During the six month period of July through December, we have allowed some employees more flexible hours since we don't need as many telephone lines available during the non tax season. This was based on seniority within our department. We also bring in employees from other units within our department to assist with the telephones so employees can schedule vacations during the summer to be with their families during the summer school break."

"The average age in our technical helpdesk contact center (250 seats) is 20 years old. We just make it a fun environment, have parties, nice incentives (movie vouchers, drinks, t-shirts) and we are very flexible in working hours and desk environment. We listen to them and use their own idea's to improve their working environment as well as the way we handle customers."

"Our contact center has only been up and running for about 5 months. We are still in the growing and learning stages. I have found, however, that flex scheduling has helped our staff tremendously. It's not easy to schedule, but it does allow the agents to alter their schedules as needed."

"We operate in an area where traffic is unbearable so we instituted a flexible tardy policy. Representatives are allowed to be tardy up to 30 minutes and if they make up the time at the end of their shift they are not counted as tardy."

"If there is no work to be done at the end of their shift, we send them home and mark their tardy excused. We deal with abusers of this policy on an individual basis. The simple fact is very few people take advantage of the program, but when necessary, it is a great tool."

"From our VOE (Voice of Employee) survey, which is done once a year, we found that employees would like to have more flexibility on time off. Based on this input, we have altered our vacation policy to an Accountability Program, which allows employees more freedom and flexibility on determining their time off. We changed our, once before, sick time to unplanned time. This program is designed for employees to be accountable for themselves and also for business needs."

"We primarily use part-time staff. The addition of full-time positions that offered health benefits was appealing. Part-time staff prefers working morning schedules. We offered more morning shifts to part-time which enabled our full-time staff to handle off phone responsibilities in the morning."

"We are located in the metropolitan DC area and have found that salary and location play a key role in attracting employees. We have trouble attracting employees because we are not convenient to public transportation. However, those employees who stay with us, do so because of the work environment. We offer a casual work place, flexible schedules and consistent non-dollar rewards. Several employees have moved from retail stores to our contact center and stress that the set schedules and relaxed atmosphere make them happy to come to work."

"We rotate our agents so that they can have a Saturday or Sunday off periodically."

"We employ a large number of part-time (college students) with very flexible hours. We also offer tuition reimbursement for some classes. Part-time employees who work 50% of their hours after regular bank hours also receive 10% shift differential. We have very little turnover in our part-time staff."

"We give our agents flexibility with their schedules. Management tells them the hours that need to be covered and the agents make up their schedule on how to do the coverage and let management know who is covering when. We do schedules a month in advance."

"Employees work fixed schedules. Early start times (usually the most sought after times) are awarded by seniority. We changed the way that vacancies are filled by offering them first to agents within our center, then going to the organization as a whole. We honored the spirit of our labor agreement and helped retain some of our most seasoned agents."

"Approximately two years ago, our CEO allowed the implementation of an initiative within our contact center that we believe is unique. To combat 50% annual turnover in a tight Atlanta job market, we took the step of reducing the workweek of contact center employees from 40 hours - to 30 hours - with the same pay! We now have less than 5% annual negative attrition and no problems attracting new job applicants. In addition - the experience level, job satisfaction, and reduction in job stress for our reps have all been impacted positively. The savings of no longer having to constantly replace reps has offset the budgetary costs of increasing our staff to make up for the hours of converting to a 30-hour workweek. We use a mix of full-time and part-time agents to counteract turnover, as well as deal with a fluctuating workload. We offer flexible hours for the part-time agents to accommodate their schedules. Our flexibility and the fact that they are not working 40 hours per week helps us avoid agent burnout and turnover."

"We adopted alternate scheduling and are pursuing the option of telecommuting. Our contact center is open 7:00 to 7:00 M-F and 8:00 to 4:30 on Saturday. Rather than working a traditional 5-day week with 8 hours per day, we adopted 3 configurations of schedules*

> traditional 5 x 8 hour days
> 4 x 10 hour days
> 4 x 9 hour days and 1 x 4 hour day.

*To meet our business needs, we excluded some days for options to choose as a day off."

"We changed our completely full-time staff to some part-time and some full-time. This allowed for greater flexibility when it came to approving time off requests. Agents felt they could ask for time off and have a reasonable chance of getting it approved. This increased loyalty and reduced turn over."

"We allow agents to retain their desired schedules after reaching a certain tenure (i.e., 1 year) versus participating in regular shift bids."

"We diversified their workday to include, not only handling incoming contacts, but also processing functions. They were able to log off during times of the day (in at least one-hour increments up to a total day) to complete other processes. As this built flexibility within our center, it also increased quality of transaction as the TSR had a more complete view of the total process. We linked this to career advancement. We got great feedback as measured by our corporate employee satisfaction surveys. FYI: To do this required a tight

153

schedule to ensure we maintained coverage during peak times."

Physical Environment

"Having the latest in furniture in the work areas is an upper for the agents."

"There is no initiative or magic bullet - it's about the basics - Make it a place where people want to work:

Coaching and follow through - are you helping them grow? Do they know what is expected of them?

Consistency and fairness - are people treated equally and with respect?

Work environment - is it a place where you would want to work everyday?

Linking the value generated to the company by the representative, to the representative's compensation.

Coupling that effort with creating a 'professional' sales environment made the difference."

Miscellaneous

"We subsidize a child care program running from early morning until late evening. We worked with a local provider to set up a center a few blocks from the office."

"We provide child care benefits. The company shares the cost with the employee of a child care facility near our call center."

"In the past, any time missed by an agent that was not pre-approved was counted against their attendance record. Recently, we changed our policy. If they are out due to illness and have sick time on the books, this time will not be counted against them."

"One of the things that we have done is develop voice applications that automate the routine inquiries that we get. Our agents can be more focused on important service issues that are generally more fulfilling types of activities. This reduces churn for us."

Hilton Hotels Uses Simulation Training to Improve Agent Performance

Hilton Reservations Worldwide is always looking for opportunities to improve the level of service it provides to its customers. When you're committed to providing the quality of service that Hilton delivers, you have to be very good at what you do.

> "When our customers call Hilton, they have come to expect a high level of service, delivered with courtesy and speed," said Carl Pollock, director of training for Hilton Reservations Worldwide. "They want to speak with someone who is professional, helpful and efficient."

So when Hilton heard about new technology with the potential to dramatically improve their training efforts, they decided to investigate. The technology was a simulation training software solution known as StarTrainer and developed by Simtrex Corporation. Designed specifically for a contact center environment, the Simtrex StarTrainer solution integrates both voice and data to create 100% true-to-life training simulations. Agents are able to listen to customers, respond to them verbally, and navigate through applications just as they would in a live call.

> "While many current training systems are capable of transferring knowledge, we wanted more than that," said Pollock. "We wanted to build employee skill to effectively handle customer interactions – without putting customer relationships at risk. Simtrex gave us the power to do that."

To determine the effectiveness of the Simtrex StarTrainer solution in its environment, Hilton conducted a study in which two groups of agents were trained simultaneously, one using traditional methods and one using the Simtrex StarTrainer solution. The results from this 12-week test showed that:

- Attrition for the StarTrainer group was 33% lower than the control group after 12 weeks

- Call handling time was 24 seconds lower immediately after training for the StarTrainer group, and remained almost 20 seconds lower than the control group after 12 weeks of on-the-job experience

- The StarTrainer group attained required performance levels 41% faster than the control group

"Once we saw the real-world results in our organizational metrics, we knew we had to move quickly to implement StarTrainer," Pollock said. "Shorter call handling times translate directly into customer satisfaction. The customer has their reservation in less time because the agent is more skilled at completing the transaction. This is a real benefit to everyone who calls Hilton."

Simtrex's StarTrainer software has now been in use at Hilton since the fourth quarter of 2000.

About Hilton Hotels Corporation

Hilton Hotels Corporation is recognized internationally as the preeminent hospitality company. The company develops, owns, manages or franchises 1,800 hotels, resorts and vacation ownership properties. Its portfolio includes many of the world's best known and most highly regarded hotel brands, including Hilton®, Doubletree®, Embassy Suites®, Hampton Inn®, Hampton Inn & Suites®, Harrison Conference Centers®, Hilton Garden Inn®, Homewood Suites®, by Hilton, Red Lion Hotels & Inns®, and Conrad International®. For more information on Hilton, please visit www.Hilton.com.

About Simtrex

Simtrex develops simulation training software for contact center operations. The Simtrex solution, known as StarTrainer, combines voice and data to replicate calls exactly as they occur in a live contact center, providing 100% true-to-life training simulations.

Unlike any other training products available today, Simtrex's StarTrainer solution simulates the actual experience of using an application and interacting with a customer at the same time. What the student sees and hears is no different from a real transaction, including the technology used to communicate. Agents are allowed to practice job skills, make mistakes, and receive mentoring from experts without jeopardizing customer relationships.

By providing real-life experience in the safety of a training environment, Simtrex gives agents both the skills and confidence to perform effectively from day one on the job. The result is decreased attrition, improved customer service, and bottom-line improvements in contact center performance.

The benefits of using StarTrainer are dramatic and proven. Simtrex customers are able to:

- *Reduce agent turnover*, through increased agent confidence and job satisfaction

- *Increase productivity*, as new agents are able to handle a normal call load much more quickly and experienced agents no longer have to be pulled from the floor to act as trainers

- *Improve consistency* by eliminating the short-cuts and undesirable procedures that are passed on through a traditional role-playing model

- *Reduce training time* because agents become proficient more quickly

Through StarTrainer, Simtrex has started a revolution in the area of contact center training. Leading companies such as AT&T, GE, and Galileo are using the StarTrainer learn-by-doing methodology to solve the compelling problem of improving the quality of customer interactions. By accelerating the experience level of contact center agents, these companies have increased their ability to achieve critical revenue and customer satisfaction objectives.

For more information about Simtrex, call 678-589-9143 or visit www.simtrex.com.

1. Ahr, P.R., Ahr, T.B., <u>Overturn Turnover</u>, Causeway Publishing Company, 2000.

2. Albertson, D., <u>Risk Assessment: Are you about to lose valuable employees</u>, Employee Benefit News, June 1, 2000.

3. ASTD – October – Nancy M. Giere.

4. Bell, C.R., Zemke, R., <u>Managing Knock Your Socks Off Service</u>, American Management Association, 1992.

5. Blanchard, K., <u>Situational Leadership</u>, Ken Blanchard Companies, 1994.

6. Block, P., <u>The Empowered Manager</u>, Jossey-Bass Inc., Publishers, 1987.

7. Branham, L., <u>Keeping the People Who Keep You in Business</u>, American Management Association, 2001.

8. Brannick, J., <u>Seven Strategies for Retaining Top Talent</u>, Journal of Business Strategy, July, 2001 v22 i4 p28.

9. Buckingham, M., Coffman, C., <u>First, Break all the Rules</u>, Simon & Schuster, 1999.

10. Covey, Stephen R., <u>Principle-Centered Leadership</u>, Summit Books, New York, 1992.

11. Dauten, D., <u>The Gifted Boss</u>, William Morrow and Company, Inc., 1999.

12. Dobbs, K., <u>Plagued by Turnover? Train your Managers</u>, Training, August 2000 v37 i8 p62.

13. Ettorre, B., How are companies keeping the employees they want? Management Review, May 1997 v86 n5 p49(5).

14. Federal Consortium, <u>Serving the American Public: Best Practices in Telephone Service</u>, Federal Government, 1995.

15. Fortune Magazine, October 3, 1994-Finding, Training & Keeping the Best Service Workers.

16. Gandy, D.B., <u>30 Days to a Happy Employee</u>, Simon & Schuster, 2001.

17. Gostick, A., Elton, C., <u>Managing with Carrots</u>, O.C. Tanner Company, 2001.

18. Greenleaf, R.K., <u>The Power of Servant Leadership</u>, Berrett-Koehler Publishers, Inc., 1998.

19. Hanson, P., <u>Why Employees Leave: The Root Cause of Employee Departure</u>, SHRM, August 21, 2001.

20. Harris, Dr. J., <u>How to Decrease Turnover and Increase Employee Retention</u>.

21. Hom, P.W., <u>Employee Turnover</u>, South-Western College Publishing, 1995.

22. IOMA's Report on Managing Customer Service, Issue 98-7, July 1998.

23. Kaye, B., Jordan-Evans, S., <u>Love 'em or Lose 'em</u>, Berrett-Koehler Publishers, Inc., 1999.

24. Kepner-Tregoe survey, Turnover: Calculating Its True Impact, Success in Recruiting and Retaining newsletter, National Institute of Business Management, December 1999.

25. Leider, Dick, <u>Intrapreneuring</u>.

26. Levering, R., Moskowitz, M., <u>The 100 Best Companies to Work for in America</u>, Bantam Doubleday Dell Publishing Group, Inc., 1993.

27. Oakley, E., Krug, D., <u>Enlightened Leadership</u>, Simon & Schuster, 1991.

28. "People Mean Profitability," a White Paper by Performix Technology, Inc.

29. Price Pritchart, <u>Service Excellence</u>, page 18 ("some jobs are tough...").

30. Rosen, R.H., <u>Leading People</u>, Penguin Books USA, Inc., 1996.

31. SHRM, <u>Why employees leave. The root cause of employee departure.</u>

32. Study of the Emerging Workforce, Saratoga Institute, Interim Service, Inc., 1995.

33. WorkUSA 2000 Study survey, <u>FAST Company</u>-Life/Work-Issue 40.

34. *Seven Strategies For Retaining Top Talent*, by Joan Brannick, "Journal of Business Strategy," July 2001.

Dr. Jon Anton (also known as "Dr. Jon") is the director of benchmark research at Purdue University's Center for Customer-Driven Quality. He specializes in enhancing customer service strategy through inbound call centers, and e-business centers, using the latest in telecommunications (voice), and computer (digital) technology. He also focuses on using the Internet for external customer access, as well as Intranets and middleware.

For the past six years, Dr. Jon has been the principal investigator of the annual Purdue University Call Center Benchmark Research. This data is now collected at the BenchmarkPortal.com Web site, where it is placed into a data warehouse that currently contains over ten million data points on call center and e-business center performance. Based on the analysis of this data, Dr. Jon authors the following monthly publications: "The Purdue Page" in *Call Center Magazine*, "Dr. Jon's Benchmarks" in *Call Center News*, "Dr. Jon's Industry Statistics" in *Customer Interface Magazine*, and "Dr. Jon's Business Intelligence" in the *Call Center Manager's Report.*

Dr. Jon has assisted over 400 companies in improving their customer service strategy/delivery by the design and implementation of inbound and outbound call centers, as well as in the decision-making process of using teleservice providers for maximizing service levels while minimizing costs per call. In August of 1996, *Call Center Magazine* honored Dr. Jon by selecting him as an Original Pioneer of the emerging call center industry. In October of 2000, Dr. Jon was named to the Call Center Hall of Fame. In January of 2001, Dr. Jon was selected for the industry's "Leaders and Legends" Award by Help Desk 2000. Dr. Jon is also a member of the National Committee for Quality Assurance.

Dr. Jon has guided corporate executives in strategically re-positioning their call centers as robust customer access centers through a combination of benchmarking, re-engineering, consolidation, outsourcing, and Web-enablement. The resulting single point of contact for the customer allows business to be conducted anywhere, anytime, and in any form. By better understanding the customer lifetime value, Dr. Jon has developed techniques for calculating the ROI for customer service initiatives.

Dr. Jon has published 75 papers on customer service and call center methods in industry journals. In 1997, one of his papers on self-service was awarded the best article of the year by *Customer Relationship Management Magazine*.

Dr. Jon has published sixteen professional books:

1. *Customer Obsession: Your Roadmap to Profitable CRM,* The Anton Press, 2002

2. *Customer Relationship Management Technology: Infrastructure for Customer Collaboration*, The Anton Press, 2002

3. *How to Conduct a Call Center Performance Audit: A to Z,* The Anton Press, 2002

4. *Integrating People with Processes and CRM Technology*, The Anton Press, 2002

5. *Selecting a Teleservices Partner*, The Anton Press, 2002

6. *20:20 CRM A Visionary Insight into Unique Customer Contact*, The Anton Press, 2001

7. *e-Business Customer Service*, The Anton Press, 2001

8. *Minimizing Agent Turnover*, The Anton Press, 2001

9. *Customer Relationship Management, The Bottom Line to Optimizing Your ROI*, Prentice Hall, 2nd Edition, 2001

10. *Call Center Performance Enhancement Using Simulation and Modeling*, Purdue University Press, 2000

11. *Contact Center Benchmarking*, Purdue University Press, 1999

12. *Listening to the Voice of the Customer*, Alexander Communications, 1997

13. *Contact Center Management by the Numbers*, Purdue University Press, 1997

14. *Customer Relationship Management*, Prentice-Hall, Inc., 1996

15. *Inbound Customer Contact Center Design*, Dame Publishers, Inc., 1994

16. *Computer-Assisted Learning*, Hafner Publishing, Inc., 1985

Dr. Jon is the editor for a series of professional books entitled *Customer Access Management*, published by the Purdue University Press.Dr. Jon's formal education was in technology, including a Doctorate of Science and a Master of Science from Harvard University, a Master of Science from the University of Connecticut, and a Bachelor of Science from the University of Notre Dame. He also completed a three-summer intensive Executive Education program in Business at the Graduate School of Business at Stanford University.

Dr. Jon can be reached at 765.494.8357 or at <DrJonAnton@BenchmarkPortal.com>.

Anita Rockwell is the Director of Business Intelligence at BenchmarkPortal, Inc. She is a Purdue University certified contact center auditor specializing in assisting contact center managers in optimally integrating people with processes and technology. Anita's primary passion is around creating the optimal environment in the contact center, with a special emphasis on the dynamics required to release the potential of each team member. In 2001, Anita co-authored a popular professional book called, "Minimizing Agent Turnover" with Dr. Jon Anton.

Anita's other core competencies include all of the following human resource challenges: 1) recruiting and screening, 2) hiring and training, 3) employee development, 4) organizational structure, 5) agent monitoring, coaching, and motivation, 6) change management, customer satisfaction surveys, and finally 7) agent quality measurement and benchmarking.

Anita has also developed a proven methodology to first discover the root causes of workflow process problems in a customer service contact center (including telephone and emails), and then to recommend specific solutions to improve efficiency and effectiveness to acceptable, best practice levels.

Anita was the Vice President of Customer Service with Simon Delivers.com where she designed, implemented, and managed an inbound customer service contact center for customer support.

Anita also spent sixteen years with the Blue Cross and Blue Shield of Minnesota where she was quickly promoted to Vice President of Customer Service, which included all aspects of customer contact management. In this capacity she was responsible for over 1 million members, 235 employees, 7 regional offices and an annual budget of over $10 million. Anita lists the following as her major accomplishments while with the Blue Cross and Blue Shield organization:

1. Re-organized the division, and championed technology enhancements.

166

2. Increased percent of inquiries resolved on first contact by 20%.

3. Increased customer satisfaction for regional service team from 75% to 87% in less than a year.

4. Dramatically reduced service employee turnover rate from over 50% to under 10% and improved employee satisfaction to a level 15% above the company average.

5. Developed and piloted first Intelligent Customer Service Workstation to streamline service delivery.

6. Increased market share in the region she managed grew from 45.5% to 49.5%.

7. Developed innovative client review tool that resulted in the identification of 250 initiatives to improve service.

8. Developed, implemented and directed one of the company's first successful pay-for-performance initiatives which increased claims productivity by over 20% while incurring no additional costs.

9. Developed processes and tools that enhanced effectiveness of the team resulting in the retention of key provider partners and turning around the satisfaction ratings of the providers with her company.

10. Worked directly with a Senior Vice President and CIO and other senior staff members on key corporate projects as part of the company's overall performance improvement strategy.

Anita graduated Cum Laude from Bethel College with a Bachelors Degree in Business Management with an emphasis in Organizational Studies. She is also currently working toward her Masters in psychology.

Anita can be reached at 651.755-1210 or at <AnitaRockwell@BenchmarkPortal.com>.

20:20 CRM A Visionary insight into unique customer contacts
By: Dr. Jon Anton and Laurent Philonenko   **Price: $24.95**
The contact center is at the heart of many businesses today, and CRM initiatives are making customer contact even more critical to the health of every company. 20:20 CRM provides a strategic view of where businesses should be going with their customer contact operation, with practical examples of how to get there.
ISBN 0-9630464-5-4

Benchmarking for Profits!
By: Bruce Belfiore   **Price: $11.95**
Done right, and done regularly, benchmarking provides improved work life, career advancement and substantially increased earnings on a consistent basis. This book is an essential manual for continuous improvement peer group benchmarking that shows convincingly why proper professionalism in today's environment requires benchmarking. Includes valuable information on how to benchmark through BenchmarkPortal and describes the latest products to help you get the most from this crucial activity.
ISBN 0-9719652-1-8

Call Center Benchmarking "How 'good' is good enough?"
By: Dr. Jon Anton   **Price: $39.95**
This "how to" book describes the essential steps of benchmarking a call center with other similar call centers, with an emphasis on "self assessment." The reader learns how to plan a benchmark, how to collect the correct performance data, how to analyze the data, and how to find improvement initiatives based on the findings.
ISBN 1-55753-215-X

Call Center Management: By the Numbers
By: Dr. Jon Anton   **Price: $46.95**
Call center technology generates reams and reams of performance data for management. Unfortunately, there is so much data that managers sometimes do not know which performance metrics are key in making decisions. This book focuses on those metrics that actually should be used in daily managment decision-making. For each metric, the reader will find a series of actions to take if the metric falls out of an acceptable, best practice, range.
ISBN 1-55753-112-9

Call Center Performance Enhancement - Using Simulation and Modeling
By: Jon Anton, Vivek Bapat, Bill Hall   **Price: $48.95**
This book provides its readers with an understanding about the role, value, and practical deployment of simulation - an exciting technology for the planning, management, and analysis of call centers. The book provides useful guidelines to call center analysts, managers, and consultants who may be investigating or are considering the use of simulation as a vehicle in their business to responsibly manage change.
ISBN 1-55753-182-X

Customer Obsession: Your Roadmap to Profitable CRM
By: Ad Nederlof and Dr. Jon Anton   **Price: $24.95**
Finally, here is a book that covers the complete "journey" of CRM implementation. Ad Nederlof and Dr. Jon Anton have done the near impossible: to position CRM in such a way that it makes practical sense to C-level executives. Beginning with the title of the book, "Customer Obsession," on through the last chapter, this book positions CRM for what it really is, namely, a complete change in corporate strategy, from the top down, that brings the customer into focus.
ISBN 0-9719652-0-X

Customer Relationship Management - Making Hard Decisions with Soft Numbers
By: Dr. Jon Anton   **Price: $55.00**
This Prentice Hall published book describes a complete methodology for driving customer feedback into executive decision-making. As the first book ever printed on CRM analytics, the reader will find unique and practical suggestions on how to make hard executive decisions using the statistics of customer perception and satisfaction, i.e., "soft numbers."
ISBN 0-13-438474-1

Customer Relationship Management Technology "Infrastructure for Customer Collaboration"
By Jon Anton and Bob Vilsoet   **Price: $39.99**
From our research on the American consumer, it has become very clear that potentially the best customer service strategy is "to offer every possible channel for the customer to help themselves, i.e., self-service." Customer actuated service is mostly driven by technology, and the "art" of self-service is to ensure that the technology is intuitive, easy to use, and that the customer is rewarded for "having done the job themselves." This book delves into all the technology solutions that enable self-service. The reader will find a robust description of the technology alternatives, and many examples of how self-service is saving companies money, while at the same time satisfying customers.
ISBN 0-9630464-7-0

Customer Relationship Management: The Bottom Line to Optimizing Your ROI
By Jon Anton and Natalie L. Petouhoff   **Price: $33.33**
Customer Relationship Management recommends effective initiatives toward improving customer service and managing change. Creative methodologies are geared toward building relationships through customer-perceived value instruments, monitoring customer relationship indices, and changing the corporate culture and the way people work.
ISBN 0-13-099069-8

e-Business Customer Service
By Jon Anton and Michael Hoeck   **Price: $44.00**
With the advent of e-business technology, we suddenly find ourselves with completely different customer service channels. The old paradigms are gone forever. This books details how to measure and manage e-business customer service. The book describes the key performance indicators for these new channels, and it describes how to manage by these new rules of engagement with specific metrics. Managing customer service in this "new age" is different, it is challenging, and it is impossible to migrate from the old to the new without reading this book.
ISBN 0-9630464-9-7

How to Conduct a Call Center Performance Audit: A to Z
By Jon Anton and Dru Phelps   **Price: $34.49**
Call centers are an important company asset, but also a very expensive one. By learning to conduct a performance audit, readers will be able to understand over fifty specific aspects of a call center that must be running smoothly in order to achieve maximum performance in both efficiency and effectiveness of handling inbound customer calls.
ISBN 0-9630464-6-2

Also available from The Anton Press

Integrating People with Processes and CRM Technology
By Jon Anton, Natalie Petouhoff, & Lisa Schwartz **Price: $39.99**
This book contains valuable information regarding the "people" side of technology initiatives. Many companies buy the best hardware and software, and spend thousands of dollars implementing technology only to find out that the employees resist the changes, and do not fully adopt the new, and possibly, improved processes. By understanding how to manage people during change, managers will see a much quicker ROI on their technology initiatives.
ISBN 0-9630464-3-8

Listening to the Voice of the Customer
By: Dr. Jon Anton **Price: $33.95**
With the help of this book, the professional skills you need to measure customer satisfaction will lead you to different approaches until you have found the one that best fits you, your company, and your organization's culture.
ISBN 0-915910-43-8

Minimizing Agent Turnover
By Jon Anton and Anita Rockwell **Price: $39.99**
Some agent turnover can be functional, but most turnover is dysfunctional and can be very expensive. This book explores the types of turnover, including internal versus external; and documents the typical causes of agent turnover. Most importantly, this book describes a methodology for diagnosing the root causes of your agent turnover, and suggests improvement initiatives to minimize agent turnover at your customer contact center.
ISBN 0-9630464-2-X

Selecting a Teleservices Partner
By Jon Anton and Lori Carr **Price: $34.99**
This book tackles one of today's hottest topics: Customer Contact Outsourcing. Companies are in a quandary about the myriad of teleservices questions they're faced with, such as deciding to outsource, cost / benefit analysis, RFP development, proposal assessment, vendor selection, contractual requirements, service level performance measurement, and managing an ongoing teleservices relationship. With the authors help, readers will find this complex issue straightforward to approach, understand, and implement.
ISBN 0-9630464-8-9

The Four-Minute Customer
By Michael Tamer **Price: $34.99**
This is a very unique book directed at developing and maintaining "Top Reps" that are uniquely motivated to deliver the highest possible quality of caller customer service at your center. Learn what it takes to find and lead the best of the best. Don't settle for mediocrity. Instead, learn how to manage the best in class customer contact center by attracting and keeping Top Reps at your organization.
ISBN 0-9630464-1-1

Order Form

Secure online ordering is available at: www.benchmarkportal.com/bookstore

Billing Information: **Shipping Information** (if different):

Billing Information	Shipping Information
Name	
Company	
Address	
Address 2	
City/St/Zip	
Phone	

Please charge my: _____ **American Express**   _____ **Discover**

                                            _____ **Mastercard**   _____ **Visa**

Card Number

Expiration Date

Signature

I've enclosed a check in the amount of

Purchase Order Number

Book Title	Amt*	Qty	Total
	Books Total		
	Shipping and Handling		
For all U.S. addresses, $5.00 for the first book, $3.00 for each additional book.			
For all International addresses, books must be **pre-paid** *and must include a shipping and handling charge of $25.00 for the first book and $10 for each additional book.*			
	Total Amount Due**		

*Call for volume and pre-order discounts available (805-614-0123 Ext. 10)

**State sales tax will be added where applicable

For other books, tapes, and videos visit our online store:

            http://www.benchmarkportal.com/bookstore

Send all orders to:

       BenchmarkPortal, Inc.

       3130 Skyway Drive, Suite 702

       Santa Maria, CA 93455-1817

For quick service, fax your order to: (805) 614-0055

For questions about your order, please call: (805) 614-0123 Ext. 10

9/10/2002